8/08

P9-DOA-391

WITHDRAWN

WITHDRAWN

OFF THE DEEP END

Also by W. HODDING CARTER

Westward Whoa: In the Wake of Lewis and Clark

A Viking Voyage: In Which an Unlikely Crew of Adventurers Attempts an Epic Voyage to the New World

Stolen Water: Saving the Everglades from Its Friends, Foes, and Florida

Flushed: How the Plumber Saved Civilization

OFF THE DEEP END

THE PROBABLY INSANE IDEA THAT I COULD SWIM MY WAY
THROUGH A MIDLIFE CRISIS — AND QUALIFY FOR THE OLYMPICS

W. HODDING CARTER

ALGONQUIN BOOKS OF CHAPEL HILL   2008

Published by
ALGONQUIN BOOKS OF CHAPEL HILL
Post Office Box 2225
Chapel Hill, North Carolina 27515-2225

a division of
Workman Publishing
225 Varick Street
New York, New York 10014

Excerpt on pp. 60–64 first appeared in *Esquire*. Portions of chapter
six were published originally in different form in *Outside* magazine.
Portions of chapter eight were published in different form in the
Kenyon College Alumni Bulletin.

Library of Congress Cataloging-in-Publication Data
  Carter, W. Hodding (William Hodding)
    Off the deep end: the probably insane idea that I could swim
  my way through a midlife crisis — and qualify for the Olympics /
  by W. Hodding Carter.
        p. cm.
    1. Carter, W. Hodding (William Hodding)   2. Swimmers —
  United States.   3. Middle-aged men — United States.
  4. Midlife crisis.   5. Olympics.   I. Title.
    GV838.C69A2 2008
    797.21092 — dc22
    [B]   2008007343

10 9 8 7 6 5 4 3 2 1
First Edition

To all those aged athletes out there with a burning
desire to kick some young butt.

OFF THE DEEP END

One

Scooping up Biohazards

I wake up with a lurch. Something hard and pointy has just jabbed me in the ribs. I'm on the very edge of my gargantuan, California king–sized bed. One tiny roll farther to my right and I'll hit the floor, not a good thing given that my right arm is not only numb but completely dead. Evidently, I've been lying on my side long enough not only to put it to sleep but also to squash whatever nerve tells it to function.

Understandably, I try rolling to my left, but there's this immovable creature there, the same thing that's poked me awake. It's my son, Angus. I crane my neck to get a view and see, of course, he's not awake, so I have to be extra quiet and tricky. It's hard getting out of bed with just one arm (I'm used to two) while also slipping a pillow along Angus's body so he'll think I'm still there. Just as I get everything in place and am about to walk away, Angus's entire body goes rigid and his knee goes crashing off to his right, directly into my wife's rear end. I'm guessing it's the same move that woke me just a minute earlier, but on Lisa, it has no effect. She lets out a fairly quiet, breath-holding snort and remains asleep. For about the two thousandth time, I wish I could sleep as soundly as she.

It's a quiet, peaceful, unusually warm fall morning for Maine's central coast. The sky is white-blue behind Mount Megunticook's silhouette. I take a few seconds to enjoy the moment, but only a few, because in a very short while, depending on who wakes up first and how, the place is going to be utter chaos.

I'm hoping to drink my creatine, do all of the ab work on my exercise ball, and write up that day's workout before Angus or any of the three girls wake up.

I'm stirring the creatine with a tall glass of fresh cider when I hear Helen scream, "I hate you, Anabel. Do you hear me? I'm never going to loan you anything again."

"Whap!" I can hear the slap from downstairs, in the kitchen. "Dad. Dad! Anabel hit me! I'm going to tell Dad, Anabel." A few minutes of banging around and a slammed door follow, and the next thing I know, Helen comes running by me, holding a pair of 7 jeans—a brand I know only because my sister bought each of our girls a pair and, ever since, they've wanted more but can't have them because they cost one hundred dollars a pair. She's going fast, probably quicker than anything I've ever seen her do when she's supposed to, like on the soccer field. A second later, Eliza comes running by, leaping past me while vainly attempting to pull Helen's hair. She misses by fractions of an inch.

"Give me back my jeans, you jerk!" Eliza demands. "Don't put your dirty hands on them. Who knows where they've been!"

"Good morning, Eliza," I try. She's caught Helen by now and is proceeding to pummel her.

"Eliza, please don't hit. Use your words." Lisa and I have been saying this to Eliza and her identical twin sister, Anabel, for nine years at least, ever since they were around two years old. It didn't work then and it doesn't work now. I try getting between them, and Eliza jerks her body, and one of her chisel-like elbows bruises my arm. "Eliza, don't get physical just because you're mad."

"I'm not doing anything, Dad. Leave me alone," she screams, grabs her jeans, and runs full tilt to the other end of the house, where Lisa and Angus are sleeping.

"Girls. Quiet!" I stage whisper.

"Dad, can you help me study my science. We have our final exam this morning," Anabel says as she saunters into the kitchen, her face as sullen as a freckly face can be.

"Didn't I ask you if you have any homework last night?" another adult asks Anabel. The voice is crackly and hoarse and it's Lisa's. She's emerged from our room, forefinger to her lips, but it does no good.

"Aaaaugh!" Helen screams. "I hate my sisters. I'm never going to loan them anything again."

"I can't believe you girls won't loan her a pair of pants," I say aloud, trying to send my voice out in a way so that A and E hear it but Angus doesn't.

"Dad! Dad! Where are you, Dad?" Angus calls from

our bedroom. He throws the door open and comes running toward the kitchen. He's been a little fixated with me the past few months and gets a tad desperate whenever he can't find me in the morning.

"Good morning, Angy. I love you," Lisa says. He smiles but makes a beeline for me, and then crashes into my thigh, perhaps accidentally rubbing green snot all over it.

"Mom, can't you quiz me?" Anabel says. "I'm going to fail."

"I gotta go," I say and start to grab my book bag. "I need to swim before my first lesson. I've got to lift today, too."

"What do you mean, go? You're joking, right" Lisa says, but I can tell from her voice that she knows I'm not joking and that she doesn't think it is funny either way. "I have court this morning at 8:30. Remember?"

"I know, I know," I say quickly. I really do remember. I just had forgotten for a few minutes, that's all. I set my bag back down. It's not a big deal. I can get my workout in after I'm done with the first lesson. "Sorry, sweetie. I love you."

"I love you, too," she replies, pushing her thick dark hair out of her face. She might be about to kiss me but the moment is lost a second later, as Angus falls off the counter while trying to reach the chin-up bar I've installed in the mudroom doorway.

❧ ❧ ❧

I don't end up getting that workout in after the first swim lesson because this is a Monday and my first lesson is followed by a second lesson, which is followed by a third.

"Hodding. What's that floating behind your back?" Casey asks. I don't immediately look behind me because I think I know what she sees, and that means trouble. Instead I sneak a quick glance at Casey. She's a five-year Y employee, head lifeguard, and my immediate charge. Seeing that I'm the assistant aquatics director and she's just the head lifeguard, I shouldn't have a sudden, overwhelming sense of guilt and fear. But I do. She has this intimidating way about her. It's not because of her height, although I'm sure she's six feet, and when she's smiling, she has the sweetest, most innocent-kid face imaginable. It's just that there's this other side to her that makes me and all the lifeguards want to make her happy. She frowns; we quake. It's that simple. The funniest thing about it is that she has no idea. She's twenty and afraid of all of us.

She's smiling. Good, maybe she has the same idea I have. This is the third lesson. As soon as it is over, I can get in my workout. I'm using one e-mailed out by my swimming guru, Mike Schmidt, and it looks like a doozy. It's got lots of kicking and a test set. I'm not sure I can handle filling and refilling my body with lactic acid this morning. I still have to do payroll.

I look behind me to see how on earth she could have seen it, to see how far it's gone, when I see cute, pudgy little Rosey, floating away—no noodle, no floaties, nothing. Is Rosey what Casey was talking about?

"Rosey, get back here this instant," I try, throwing in a hearty laugh just in case I've sounded too rough. Too late. She starts to wail.

Now how am I going to do this? The thing I am worried Casey might see is not Rosey but instead floating feces, what we call in the business a "biohazard." It's leaked out of the suit of a girl who is over four. The fact that she's four is why it's leaked out in the first place. If she were only three and eleven-twelfths, all would still be okay because she would be wearing a plastic pull-up. We require all children under four to wear such swimming attire, but, of course, even older kids can make mistakes. I've seen seemingly normal grown-ups release a biohazard or two so I'm in no way upset with this little girl. It's just that if Casey or anybody else who knows what they're doing sees it, then there goes my workout for the day. The state code that covers public swimming areas mandates that such organic matter, along with other bodily fluids including but not limited to vomit and blood, be removed from the pool and that the pool then be "shocked," whereby the attendant raises the level of chlorine in the pool from the usual two parts per million to twenty (a concentration potent enough to bleach hair and deadly to all microbial life forms). The pool must stay at this lethal level for at least twelve hours. In other words, the pool gets closed and Hodding doesn't get to train.

Desperation doesn't come close to what I'm feeling, and I'm just about to scoop the Baby Ruth bar – size poop up with my hand and stuff it under my Speedo as I lunge toward Rosey, who appears to be turning onto her stomach — a place she is very, very uncomfortable with — when a sudden, unexpected wave of responsibility rolls over me. Or maybe it's just revulsion. Either way, instead of tucking away the biohazard as I catch Rosey's leg and stop her from rolling, I blow my whistle three times and yell, "Clear the pool!" loud enough not only to get the attention of everyone whose head is above water in the main pool but also to alert people over in the therapy pool more than one hundred feet away.

Casey looks at me, her brow broken with worry, and then just as quickly, she's scanning the pool, looking for the body.

"It's just a poop," I tell her quickly and then point to it as it swirls past my hip. I hand Rosey to one of the Y staffers in charge of the nursery kids and hop out. Casey looks disgusted and gets out right behind me. While she goes over and stops the swimmers and reassures some of the elderly people who've been startled awake by my whistle and scream, I scoop up the offender in a net, shaking my head at how such a lowly thing could wield so much power.

I don't have enough time to begin the shocking treatment, so I leave it for Casey, which is definitely a good thing for the pool. Last time I messed with the chemicals, a twelve-hour shutdown turned into a thirty-six-hour one. I'd used measurements meant for the main pool in the therapy pool, which holds about a quarter of the volume.

I need to run to my next class, but since that would be breaking pool rule number two — no running — (number one is no swimming without a lifeguard; tellingly, as far as the modern pool-supervising culture goes, most of our rules are phrased in the negative), I employ the stride of an Olympic walker, a technique I feel I've gotten pretty good at in the seven months I've been working at the Y. Along the way, Grace hands me a bag. She and her mom have made me a loaf of banana bread. The card reads: "I am thankful you teach me. Love, Grace."

A group of women mostly over sixty in all shapes and sizes gathers near the water slide. A couple smile at me as I approach, while the rest listen earnestly to the woman with dyed-auburn hair.

"She said she was only going to have the one knee done but the doctor told her she'd be wasting her time if she didn't just go ahead and replace both of them. I don't think she'll be . . ."

"Hi, ladies!" I exclaim, forcing an unnaturally wide grin to cross my face. I've been told that I don't smile enough when I'm running my Liquid Toning class, which is an intermediate-level water aerobics class. "Let's get going."

I never in my life imagined that I would teach a water aerobics class. In truth, I had always considered them a joke, even more ridiculous than land-based aerobics. But not only have I grown better at teaching it — at least according to the ladies, who let me know every single thing I do wrong—but I actually enjoy it. In fact, and this is difficult to admit, it's one of my favorite classes in the week. I've been teaching the same group since I started the job in April 2007. I know about Anne's back and Lyme disease, Caroline's tricky shoulder and enviable trip through the Panama Canal, Gloria's upcoming knee operation. (Names have been changed to protect me.) They've seen me go from the guy who counted like a metronome to the guy who . . . well, I still count like a metronome but I've improved in other areas. I couldn't remember the difference between the rocking-horse move and the frog leaps to save my life and I'd leave out five exercises one week and pretend that I was doing it on purpose so I could add new stuff. Only problem was, I didn't come up with anything new that day.

The class takes forty-five minutes. First we walk back and forth across the fifteen-yard-wide, eighty-seven-degree pool. I yell out the different moves—anything from "ice skating" to "ballerina toes"—and worry that I'm developing a lisp. I know it's not fair, but it just seems like the kind of class a more effeminate man might enjoy teaching. So what does it mean about me? I have to remember not to wear my Speedo next class but instead my long surfer shorts. Much cooler.

Next we do our stretches. I stand in the shallow end and they stand in the deeper water facing me. Everything is loud and bubbly until we get to the hip-rotating exercise. I hold my hands on my hips and gyrate in a pretty suggestive manner. They all grow quiet, not just this time but every time.

"What? What am I doing?" I ask.

"It's Jason," Alaina says. "We liked the way he did it." And there I am, thinking they were quiet because I'm so sexy. Maybe I don't like the class so much after all. Jason was my predecessor—the twenty-one-year-old love of everybody's life who tricked me into thinking this job would be easy and would give me plenty of time to train for the Olympics.

After stretching, it's time for the aerobic part of the class. We jog, jump, stride, rotate our arms, push Styrofoam dumbbells in all sorts of maneuvers above and below the water while jogging—all in an effort to get their hearts doing better than one hundred beats per minute. We're supposed to do some abdominal exercises with a floating noodle and then squeeze in one more round of stretching before I send them on their way but when I'm teaching, it never happens. Today, our time is up even before we finish with the dumbbells. I'm about to add one more exercise when Glenda walks into the pool.

Glenda is here for her arthritis class and is taller and stronger than I am. She's scowling, and even though she no longer thinks I'm the lamest employee in the lot, I decide not to push it.

"Hi, Glenda," I say.

"How's the path to Beijing going?" she asks. "I want to go with you, if you make it."

"You got it," I say, and I mean it, if there's a way to do

it. Maybe it's the constant assault on my senses by the overwhelming heat and noxious chlorine smell or maybe it's just from shared time at the Y but I really like these ladies. I'll take them all with me, if I make it there.

Hour after hour my day goes on like this. I squeeze in an extra-hard session on the weights. Usually I swim for one and a half hours as well but the biohazards put an end to that. No matter, I'll do extra yardage tomorrow. Guards call in claiming that they haven't been able to find anyone to cover their shift, which just so happens to be in less than an hour. One girl actually calls thirty minutes before her shift to tell me she's quitting.

"It just hasn't worked out," she explains. "I've got too much school work right now and I really believe I have to put my priorities there." I tell her it's okay and hang up. Then I pump my fist in celebration. Her retirement means one less headache. She has never shown up to work her shift. Not once. My boss, Jen, the aquatics director, hasn't returned from maternity leave yet so handling these things falls in my lap and I worry for the umpteenth time how distraught she's going to be when she returns. I'm a horrible supervisor.

Even though the main pool is closed, people keep trickling in all evening long. I was supposed to leave at 5:30 but the night supervisor has called in sick. Casey and I flipped a coin. I lost.

Tyler, the new guard, and I go through the ritual of closing the pool. We collect water samples, drop in the re-agents, and write down the chlorine and pH levels. We hose down the entire deck because the upper gutters have a water trap so shallow that the water will evaporate out of it in twenty-four hours, leaving the pool area smelling like a sewer. I send Tyler home and then I lock the locker room doors so nobody can slip in and drown while the pool is closed, turn off the lights, and head for home. It's eight p.m.

On the way out, Peter, a new kid on the swim team I'm coaching, stops me, but at first, he doesn't say anything.

"Yes, Peter," I try to prompt him. "You stopped me."

"Coach," he says, swinging his head from side to side, looking me in the eye and then not, his chlorine-bleached bangs almost obscuring his view. "Is it true you're going to the Olympics? That's awesome. Really awesome."

Now it's my turn not to look him in the eyes. I smile and look down at the ground. "We'll see, Peter. We'll see," I almost stammer. "But I'm definitely trying."

Two

Saggy Old-Man Butt

In February 2004 I decided I was going to qualify for the Olympics.

I was forty-one.

At that age, most men who are suddenly afraid of yet one more day flying by buy motorcycles or get twenty-year-old girlfriends or they doctor up their bodies with pectoral implants — some even do all three. The majority, however, don't abruptly decide to pit themselves against the greatest swimmers in the world.

What was I thinking? I could draw attention away from my mostly unsuccessful life? Maybe. I'd been a professional writer for nearly fifteen years but had recently failed to make minimum wage. I had always known that by this point in my career I would have already published a best seller and I'd be coasting along on royalties and movie deals. After all, my first book had a decent mention in the *New Yorker* and Dick Clark Productions offered to turn it into a movie. But instead of those early successes being stepping stones to the pinnacle of modern author-hood, they were my most triumphant moments. Hard as I tried, I wasn't Jon Krakauer. And my latest book had sold so disappointingly that I was considering giving up writing. And, more importantly, my wife and I had hit bumpy terrain, nearly derailing the marriage. Certainly, I needed a fix, and swimming had always done its part in the past, helping me through the sketchier times of my life. So perhaps that's all it was: an unreflective fix to a faltering life.

I remember the fateful day as if it changed the course of my life—because, of course, it did. We had a new YMCA in town and the pool's chlorinated waters lapped at my heart like a long-lost friend. I slipped in, jumping along the bottom in my ill-fitting Speedo (I refused to wear any size but the one I'd had in college). A small fold hanging over the top of the suit jiggled impatiently as I tried to warm up. At first, my arms felt awkward, what I imagine a young colt might feel as he exits his mother's womb or better yet, an old worn-out bear as he lumbers out of hibernation. In other words, I didn't feel so hot. But as I piled on the laps and let my body adjust to these barely recalled demands, I started to feel stronger and stronger. Instead of suffocating me both literally and figuratively, the water buoyed my body and spirit. I was grinning by lap forty.

Not wanting to push things but feeling a slight tingle in the back of my neck, I got out after only a mile of easy swimming. But as I drove home, consciously tucking that aforementioned fold into my Levi's, a small thought—

what if?—wandered into my head. I quickly batted it aside so as not to jinx things. After a few more days of easy swimming, however, and a couple of practice sets similar to ones I'd done in college, I felt a twenty-year hiatus[1] slip away like money at the fairway. Most important to this story, I felt fast—so fast that I believed I could qualify for that summer's Olympic Trials—although I hadn't even done so at the top of my game in 1984.

And that's how it started. I wrote to a friend at *Esquire* magazine, got an assignment to write my aquatic version of *The Rookie*,[2] and lighted out to get myself to the Olympics, one meet at a time. The first of which was

1. It was actually only a seventeen-year hiatus but the roundedness of twenty sounds better. Also, I was reluctant to mention the exact figure because I thought the fact that I tried this qualify-for-the-Olympics-after-a-long-break thing in 1987 after my stint in the Peace Corps might scare off the more casual reader. He/she might get the idea that I'm some sort of Olympic-wannabe nutjob and would drop this book before really giving it a chance. But I know that if you're bothering to read this footnote, you're giving me a chance. So, yes, I did try this once before, right after working in Kenya for two years, and I did fail that time. There were a lot of reasons for that failure, including the fact that I was training with a bunch of twelve-year-olds and I was twenty-four. Also, I still had giardia, which required me to spend more time in the bathroom than in the pool.

2. My kids and I watch it—the Dennis Quaid movie where he plays a forty-plus rookie ballplayer who never got to take his chance when he was a kid—all the time for obvious reasons. They, in fact, know it so well they fast-forward through all the parts that make me cry. Although I'm not really making a comeback because I'm really just trying to make it for the first time, I like thinking of myself as being spiritually connected with Dennis Quaid (or his character, I guess, to be more precise).

the New England Masters Championships at Harvard, a meet I entered just so I could amuse myself by competing against a bunch of mostly elderly guys (actually, they were my age, older, and younger—anywhere between nineteen and dead).

I trained furiously for six weeks, replicating, to some extent, my old college workouts and eating habits. "To some extent" meant just that—to some extent. I couldn't do the really hard sets we'd pulled off in college, or if I did, I could manage three repeats of a given interval as opposed to the ten I could handle back then. And, more to the age-related point, I worked hard only every other day. I learned the hard way that it takes a forty-year-old body nearly twice as long to recover from a hard workout than it takes a twenty-year-old body. I didn't know this from research. I knew it because I could hardly drag my lazy butt down to the Y the day after I'd worked out hard. Of course, my wife, Lisa, noticed this immediately, asking one morning as I rushed out the door leaving her to handle all four kids only minutes after they'd awoken (yet again), "Does Michael Phelps work out only three times a week?"

She was probably just getting me back for the meals. Although I wasn't working out day after day like I used to, I was burning off an extra two to three thousand calories a day. To make up for it, I devoured meals full of protein, fat, and carbs all day long and I'd ask questions such as, "Am I losing too much weight?" This didn't go over so well with Lisa, but what could she say?[3] I was trying to fulfill a dream.

And I hit the weights hard, doing the same dry-land routine I'd done my senior year. It was probably the weights that had convinced me that I would be able to do as well as I had in college. I'd never really stopped lifting (except for that short period in the early nineties when I had a couple of burst fractures in my spine and couldn't get out of bed for a third of a year) and could already bench more than I had in college. When it came to weights, I'd been the proverbial ninety-seven-pound weakling from the back page of the comic books while in college, so lifting more than I could then wasn't saying much, necessarily, but it was true. I could now easily bench two hundred pounds and whip off twenty dips in a row.

With one and a half hours in the gym and up to two in the pool every other day, I wasn't the quintessential family man, but I was toughening up.

Bring it, I thought.

To this day, I cringe when I recall that weekend at Harvard—not so much the hubris (though there was plenty of that) but the pain. There was so much of it.

Before an important competition, swimmers change their routine by going into a workout phase called "taper."

3. Well, she could say things like, "If you don't stop buying whoopee pies and deep-frying anything you can lay your hands on, I'm moving out. I can't even eat with the rest of you anymore!"

In a nutshell, tapering is simply cutting back on the amount swum in a practice while increasing or improving the quality. As you get closer and closer to the meet, you reduce by more and more yardage, so that within a few days of the competition, you are swimming only just enough to warm up your muscles and keep your feel for the water. I didn't taper before this meet because I was saving that for a few weeks later, in preparation for when I'd swim in another meet[4] to qualify for the Olympic Trials in Long Beach, California. But even without tapering, I just knew I'd be swimming very fast—certainly faster than any of the old farts at a Masters Championship.

I've blocked out much of that weekend from my memory, but I do recall warming up the first morning of the meet, feeling pretty good. I was clearly feeling cocky; I'd even booked a room at one of the more expensive hotels recommended by the meet directors, knowing that soon I'd have so many sponsors that cost wouldn't mat-

4. I would gladly have tapered for this meet but I hadn't really been swimming long enough to do so. In other words, I didn't really have anything to taper off. Plus this annual competition is held in a short course yard pool as compared to the Olympic-length pools, which are called long course meter pools. It gets a little confusing because there are three different types of swimming race courses: the two I've mentioned—short course yard pools and long course meter pools—and short course meter pools. Short course yard pools are twenty-five yards long and are used in most U.S. high school and college competitions. Long course meter pools are fifty meters long and are used for Olympic and most world competitions. Short course meter pools are twenty-five meters long and used the world over, although they're not all that popular in the United States.

ter. When I did a few practice 50s — two lengths of the pool swum at the rate I expected to swim my actual race (which was, actually, four times as far, something I might have taken into account) — I was right on target. According to the pace clock, I was covering fifty yards in twenty-five seconds. I did the math: add four of those together, subtract two seconds for the advantage that a racing dive would give me, and I'd do it in 1:38, just a few tenths off the time I would need to qualify for the Trials.[5] This was going to be like stealing a walking stick from your grandpa — apt, given who was in the pool with me. I'd never seen so many gray beards, ill-fitting Speedos, and human sausages in a single pool. This last image comes courtesy of the sight of overweight men and women squeezed into tech suits — those full-length bodysuits that Michael Phelps and others wear at major competitions.[6] I laughed at all these elderly swimmers investing

5. I'd converted meters to yards to get this time. The time for the trials was actually for the 200-meter freestyle and as I've pointed out, this competition was in a short course yard pool. I was swimming two hundred yards. A decent male swimmer generally goes fifteen seconds faster in the 200-yard freestyle because of the shorter distance and increased number of turns. A properly performed flipturn gives your arms a break and, thanks to the push off, propels you faster than you can swim.
6. I could easily write an entire book on the subject of these suits. Some people rant that they should be made illegal. Others swear they do no good—that it's all advertising. The reason they're called "tech suits" is because they represent a technological breakthrough and are designed from scientific research. I believe Speedo was the first to come up with these suits, offering

hundreds of dollars in a swimsuit that could improve one's time by only mere fractions of a second.

So, there I was, feeling quite pleased with myself. In less time than it would've taken me when I was in my supposed "prime," I'd not only returned to racing form but was about to exceed all expectations. Did they still put athletes on Wheaties boxes or should I just try for one of those Gap print ads? I wondered. Could I be a pro and swim at the Olympics?

---

something they called a Fastskin. The claim was that it (and its descendants) did things that no suit had ever done before. The fabric shed water, it floated (instead of sinking like the stuff in most suits), it compressed muscle, making for faster, stronger contractions, it got rid of flabby skin, etc. The Fastskin II even claimed to have a surface similar to "shark dentricles." I have no idea what that means, but it sure does sound fast. There are studies out there conducted by coaches—in which swimmers are dragged by a machine at the same velocity whether wearing the suit or not, for instance—proving that the suits work. There are also studies out there proving that they don't. You simply had to choose your study and go with it. I chose the "they work" study out of desperation and because the coach at Auburn, David Marsh, who has done studies, told a friend who asked, "You need to get one." If the man coaching the fastest swimmers in the country says get one, then I'm going to get one. Are they ethical? Right now, they're legal, but many say that's simply because Speedo has invested so much money into their research that FINA, the world governing body for swimming, had to accept them. The only thing I find horrible about them is their price—up to four hundred dollars—and their Apple-style merchandising. Every year, a new model comes out that makes the previous year's model obsolete. I love Speedo's latest, the Fastskin Pro. It makes me feel like some kind of superhero.

If I'd been honest with myself, I would've realized that the fact that I'd done only two 50s and had rested a few minutes between each one meant that they weren't true indicators of my pace. If I'd been honest with myself, I would've swum four of them with only ten seconds rest between each one. Or I might have taken note of the fact that I was completely winded after each 50, and that my jaw ached from the lactic acid etching its way through my muscles. All of which should have been signs, but I wasn't seeing signs that day. I was just there to kick some saggy old-man butt.

A few hours later, after I'd recovered from the warm up, I dove in for the actual race, laughing to myself at the thought of these old guys about to be decimated by the Mississippi Dark Horse. I was suddenly that same skinny, freckle-faced boy from the Mississippi Delta who always knew he'd swim fast enough to qualify for the Olympic Trials. Finally, here I was about to do the unthinkable at age forty-one with barely any training to speak of. Imagine how fast I would swim just a few weeks later after a proper taper!

❍ ❍ ❍

All of us who have ever played a sport with some degree of coordination have, at some point, dreamed of being an Olympian. For me, it had been (and clearly still was) an obsession. I was a weak kid with a strong imagination and I could feel the weight of the gold medals and hear the unreachable notes of our national anthem nearly every night before drifting off to sleep. I knew that someday my face would be plastered in the history books, right alongside Johnny Weissmuller, Shane Gould, and Mark Spitz.

And so I swam, day after day, year after year, mostly plodding along without anything to back up my wildest dreams except countless laps in the pool. Some summers I would log ten miles a day (an effort equal to forty miles running). Others, I would swim more laps of butterfly than most swimmers would do in a lifetime. I went to swim camps. My parents bought me a set of Sears free weights. I drank gallons of Nutrament. I read *Swimming World* from cover to cover. I bought and read books on swimming technique that most of my coaches hadn't even bothered to look at. I genuflected before my sister's life-size poster of Mark Spitz. Yet I still sucked. My best showing was second place at the Mississippi state championships in the 50 fly when I was ten years old — behind Frankie Franklin of CST (the Columbus Swim Team), who seemed to take great pleasure in calling me Carter Farter every time we met.

It wasn't until my senior year at Kenyon College, the perennial powerhouse in NCAA Division III swimming, that all the dreaming paid off. Almost. After a transformative year in which Coach Jim Steen tricked me into becoming the swimmer I wanted to be, I not only qualified for Nationals in three individual races but I took second place in the 200 freestyle and won gold medals on two relays. My time in the 200 even qualified me to compete at Division I Nationals and was only a second or so off the Olympic Trials standard. The Mississippi Kid was finally going to get his gulp of golden air. At twenty-one, I'd finally figured out the best way for me to train and I knew that with just a few more months of such swimming, I'd be able to make that cut. All I'd have to do is keep swimming for four more years—until the 1988 Olympics.

It was summer and I was living in New Orleans with my mom, who had moved there after my parents' divorce. I'd squeaked by with a degree in English literature and, miracle of miracles, I'd been accepted as a Peace Corps volunteer. In September, I was supposed to go to Kenya to teach English. That was the plan, but now I wanted to change it. I just needed a few more months to prove my Olympic potential.

My father, visiting for the weekend, and I were driving down St. Charles Avenue on a sticky, sultry evening. Just walking from the car to a restaurant was enough to put a person in a bad mood. Maybe picking this moment to announce my reversal wasn't the best timing. I was slouched in the backseat of my dad's car and my friend Stephen Chung was sitting in the front, his face red from too much wine, muttering something about rednecks, barbecue, and Texas oil.

"Dad, remember how amazing it was when I swam so fast at Nationals—dropping all that time out of the blue?" I asked. "I'm thinking I should keep on swimming now that I'm finally going so fast. Train for four more years, wait tables maybe, and qualify for the 1988 Olympics. I read somewhere that I can defer the Peace Corps."

If I remember correctly, he slammed on the brakes, Chung thudded against the vinyl dashboard, and I quickly realized he wasn't too keen on the idea.

"Damn it, Hodding," he said, spinning around, his right hand slapping hard on the back of the passenger seat. "No way." His face flushed dark red and his lips were pinched tight—definitely not the way I liked seeing him. The last time I could remember him getting so angry in a car was when eleven-year-old David Weiss, about to lose in a vicious game of cows (you know—you count the cows on your side of the car, your opponent counts the ones on his side, horses are worth half a cow), covered my dad's eyes so he couldn't count. The main problem with David's move, at least from my dad's point of view, was that my dad was driving. "It's time for you to grow up."

"But you always said a Marine never gives up," I reminded him. He'd done ROTC in college and had always seemed quite fond of this expression, at least when I wanted to quit doing something he wanted me to do. Time and again, he'd used it to urge me to attend yet one more practice. "I've finally got a shot. I'm so close."

"You also need to know when to move on," he answered without missing a beat. "You've dicked around too much. You're going into the Peace Corps."

And that was that. Although I was twenty-one and technically, I could do whatever I wanted, I possessed a well-groomed guilt. My father had paid for my whole life up to this point and bankrolled those countless summer days when I swam five hours daily but did nothing else. I'd had only one real summer job my entire spoiled life, and my time had finally come to do something other than swim.

"Okay," I answered meekly and put my quest aside.

Until now. Finally, it was my turn—again.

I was still chuckling to myself by the end of the first lap; I was clearly out in front and these old fogeys were going *down*. After the first 50, things started to get ugly. I pushed off the wall, expecting my hands to be locked together, one on top of the other, my arms stretched out, slicing through the water like an arrowhead—what we swimmers call perfect streamline—but no such luck. Instead, they were quaking like rubbery Gumby limbs. I took a stroke as I rose to the surface and instantly I knew the entire venture had been a colossal mistake. My heretofore-powerful left arm felt like it belonged to some weak mama's boy. My right could do no better. Did I start to cry? No, but not because I didn't want to. I simply didn't have enough energy. By the 100, when all those "old farts" started to pass me by, I did let out a small scream. My limbs began to burn as they filled with lactic acid and I worried I might not stay afloat, never mind finish each increasingly painful stroke. Suddenly I thought my dad's advice twenty years earlier had been quite wise. In fact, if I lived through this race, I was never going to swim again.

By the time I touched the wall at the 200-yard mark, my feet and hands had turned a sickening yellow-white from lack of circulation (my heart and lungs had co-opted every-thing for survival's sake), and I had to crawl not only out of the pool but along the deck to the back wall so I could make room for the next heat of old men—all of whom beat me soundly. I huddled back there for a good half hour unable to do anything but breathe.

It was suddenly clear to me: I should quit and give up this idea. But I had one small problem: my wife and chil-dren were driving down from our home in Maine to see me race. When I got back to my hotel room, I frantically called to tell her not to come, but it was too late. They were less than an hour away.

I had to finish what I was now referring to as my Swim of Shame. The next day, I competed in the 100 free—a shorter and ostensibly easier race. I don't remember much about that swim except for two things. One was that I ne-glected to check in on time and so I had to race with a group of eighty-year-old men. The other was a conversation I had after the race. Twenty-two minutes after, to be precise. I re-member how many minutes it'd been since the race because every thirty seconds or so, I glanced at my watch to see how long I'd been breathing at a rate faster than a birthing mother. I hadn't really thought it was possible to breathe so rapidly for so long without passing out and, in fact, that's what I felt like I was going to do at any moment, even though I'd made my way into the men's locker room and was sitting down with my head between my legs.

It was very quiet in the locker room, eerily so—as if all the other men were wondering the same thing as I:

exactly when was I going to die. At twenty-two minutes and thirty seconds, the gentleman who had been racing next to me came in and broke the silence. He put aside his walker, set his hand firmly on my shoulder, and said with the surety of one who'd been there: "Don't worry. It gets better after a while."

I wasn't so sure.

Three

The Race Club

After that early, miserable experience racing at Harvard—when I lost circulation in my hands and feet and was unable to catch my breath—I did the most sensible thing I could think of. I quit. As much as I wanted to suck in the polluted air of Athens from the confines of the Olympic Village, it clearly wasn't going to happen. And if I couldn't race against Michael Phelps and Gary Hall Jr., I wasn't going to swim at all. What was the point?

That kind of thinking lasted about a year. But no matter how bold a picture reality painted, I refused to believe that just because I was a little older, I couldn't swim as fast as I used to. I'd been so close—just some twenty years ago—I had to give it one more try.

I'd reignited my love affair with water. I've always associated swimming with freedom. And joy. And youth. Set me at the edge of a body of water and I know—no matter how turbid, rough, or expansive that realm might be, I can escape—like Horatius, the savior of Rome, swimming to shore after defending the bridge against the Etruscans. As long as the water runs deep, I can go where most others can't follow. Free myself of this earthly baggage — shrug off our mortal condition for as long as my body can stay immersed — minutes, hours, sometimes half a day, even. For me, swimming, or just floating in water, feels like a drop of immortality. It has been that way for as long as I can remember. I love swimming, the feel of the water swirling past my body, the different forces exerted on the palm of my hand as I stroke through the water, the gentleness of being buoyant. Swinburne, an overly passionate Victorian poet, described the "sacred" sea as "paradise lost . . . another and better world" where a person "lived and moved and had one's being." What a perfect place to be transported to just as I was realizing that life wasn't going to go on and on forever and ever.

Swimming had been my constant companion from adolescence on. The first time I kissed a girl was in the back of a station wagon at an out-of-town swim meet. When I had a full-blown anxiety attack in college, swimming put me back on my feet. It had landed me my first national magazine assignment — an article about Mark Spitz. In short, being a swimmer was how I'd defined myself for more than half my life. That initial return to swimming might have been a midlife fancy, but given swimming's position in my life's hierarchy, how could I turn my back on this challenge, this chance to prove that I didn't have to grow old? Where else could this path travel but through the water? I had to go on and see this thing through to the end. I missed swimming. Plain and simple.

And more importantly, my marriage was looking a bit rockier than before—we were talking about living in separate homes—and my career, well, at that point, it seemed like there wasn't one. I hadn't written for a magazine all year.

So in January 2005 I dove back into the nurturing warmth of the YMCA pool. Lo and behold, after a few repeat 100s, I once again decided that I was going to qualify for the Olympics. In retrospect, I had no business thinking that feeling good while swimming 100s at a 1:20 pace made me Beijing worthy, but to my everlasting confusion, it did. There was something about the way I felt—comfortable, comforted, perhaps like a tiger just before it pounces—that told me, with a lot of work, I could make it.

I started training again—like a fiend. Lifting weights. Reading a dictionary-like tome by Ernie Maglischo called *Swimming Fastest*. Covering three miles a day in the pool, six days a week.

I'd wake up in the morning, make the kids' breakfast, and down a gloppy mixture of creatine, whey protein, yogurt, and whatever else I could lay my hands on. Once the kids were off to school and Lisa and I had finished arguing about why I hadn't thrown my dirty socks, shirt, underwear, and pants in the dirty-clothes basket instead of on the floor, I'd drive over to the Y and lift for about an hour. Then I'd rush down to the pool and, after no warm-up, I'd start swimming while attached to a bungeelike tether, tied to a starting block. The farther I swam, the stronger it pulled me back to the wall. It was an exhausting, futile exercise because the bungee cord always won and eventually pulled me back. But my heartrate was well over 190 and my arms felt like they'd been beaten by an angry mob. Next, I'd go off to the library to write, but instead I'd fall asleep for an hour or so. After lunch, I'd return to the Y and swim for another hour and a half. Later, I'd meet up with Lisa back home and we'd greet the kids getting off the bus. All I'd want was to sleep but we still had dinner to make and stories to read the kids to sleep with. I'd pass out around 8:30 and then do it all over again the next day.

Shortly, though, everything collapsed. Lisa and I had to sell the house because the renovations that I had insisted we make cost about $200,000 too much and we couldn't pay our mortgage. For some reason, I'd thought it very necessary to have a local cabinetmaker construct longleaf yellow pine cabinets with hand-planed panels and wide, black walnut counters. Alone, they cost us more than $25,000 to fill a space that a decent array of Home Depot cabinets would have filled for about $3,000. We were also broke because I wasn't writing because I'd convinced myself that my book on the Florida Everglades[1] was going to

1. The Everglades is a wide, swampy river that the sugar industry and the state of Florida have destroyed and the federal government has said it is restoring but has never bothered to follow up on. The U.S. Army Corps of Engineers and the Florida legislature have continued to use the supposed restoration as the main component of a get-rich-quick land-development scheme. If you want to know more, get in touch with me, and I'll send you a copy of my book. I think copies are hard to find. For some reason, it's no longer in print.

be embraced as the successor not only to Marjory Stoneman Douglas's ode *The Everglades: River of Grass* but also to all of Bruce Chatwin's works. My Everglades rumination was going to rocket to the top of the best-seller list and I was never going to have to work again. That didn't happen. As a result of my free spending on the house and for various other reasons (the dirty clothes, my need to be right no matter what, my having left Lisa alone with our toddler twins and newborn daughter a few years earlier for a total of seven months while I went off sailing a replica Viking ship, hogging all the attention — do I have to go on?), Lisa and I tried living apart for a while.

I need a lot of attention and praise and Lisa needed a break from holding me up while simultaneously feeling like the third wheel in our family. I didn't realize these were the issues at the time, of course, nor did I immediately try to do anything about them, or else, of course, we wouldn't have been having problems. At first, it was a painful (but informative) time for both of us, but we kept our focus on the kids: their routines remained as much the same as we could manage — we both put them to bed, we both were there in the mornings, and we still ate most meals together. It was hard on them, but since we tried to keep their lives stable and consistent, we like to think it was less damaging than it could've been.

Our marriage survived, but for a while my swimming didn't. I stopped going to the pool with any consistency in March 2004 and didn't start up again for real until the fall of 2005.

To mark the day and keep myself honest, I began a diary, something I've always done when on a mission or quest. An excerpt from my first entry provides a pretty good glimpse into that less-than-pretty time in my life:

November 9, 2005 This morning, while lying in bed, rubbing my lats, I remembered that the sports massage therapist I saw last summer, after hearing my goal and why I was coming to him, suggested I see a shrink. I was so focused at the time that I didn't even think to be insulted. Ah, I'm filled with such confidence.

I wish the pool was about two degrees warmer. And I wish I could say I was doing something exceptional in the pool right now but I'm not. And (yes, another and) I'm not even sure that the claim that my max heart rate is 200 or 220 (or whatever I recently claimed) is really true. The highest I've gotten it lately is 180. But then I keep telling myself that I'm not in good enough shape yet to really test it out. I think that's probably true. I'm gonna go swim now. Oh yeah. I looked at a piece of property with Uncle Phil two days ago that could fit Lisa and

me in separate houses no problem—if
we had a little money to build houses,
but since all we have is the $165,000
that is left over from the sale of our
home, I don't see how we can do it.

I don't know if it was writing down my goals in a diary or things getting better with Lisa—counseling helped us hear each other for the first time in quite a while, although time, more than anything, healed us—but after starting back that fall, I didn't quit swimming ever again.

Yet even with a more consistent approach to my training, I wasn't seeing the results I wanted, and by the winter of 2006, as taper time for the New England Masters Championships approached, I realized I needed a boost to my training. Swimming with Dolly, my seventy-four-year-old training partner, just wasn't going to be enough. While I appreciated her suggestions that my straight-arm recovery on my right side was throwing off my stroke's rhythm, I felt I needed a few more eyes on the situation. Dolly was one tough lady. Shipped over here from Austria as an infant during World War II, raised in an orphanage and then by foster parents, and struck down with polio, she'd managed to survive it all. It might take her almost a minute to cover a length of the pool doing butterfly, but she was far stronger than I'd ever be. Also, she was almost always right about the flaws in my stroke. In one afternoon, as she tried to keep apace of me, walking on the pool deck as I sprinted one-length butterflies, she corrected the way I'd swum fly my entire life. But Dolly's inner strength wasn't rubbing off on me and I sorely needed some help.

One night after Lisa and I had moved both of our households into our new, much cheaper home, and the kids had all been read to and I was nodding off before the computer but still searching for some kind of answer to my swimming conundrum, I happened upon the Web site for something called the Race Club—home to the winningest 50 freestyler in history: Gary Hall Jr.

Gary Hall Jr. has won gold medals in three Olympics and is the second fastest swimmer ever. The fastest is Hall's Russian nemesis, Aleksander Popov, who once said to him before a race, "I'm going to kick your Yankee ass because you're soft."[2] If anybody could get me swimming faster, it had to be Gary and his camp staff. Plus, it was practically the only swim race camp out there for adults. The U.S. Masters Association ran a week-long camp at the Olympic Training Center in Colorado Springs, Colorado, but I'd already missed it. An open-water guru named Terry Laughlin owned a company that operated clinics all around the United States, but I wasn't interested in learning how to swim long and strong—his specialty. I wanted speed. And the only other camp I could find was offered by some company calling itself Somax. As their

2. Popov was a ruthless competitor when it came to talking trash about Gary. He was always challenging him, and once, after beating him in a preliminary round, said he was going to continue beating Gary because he came from a family of losers.

Web site explains, their name is from the Greek, *soma,* meaning "body," and I wasn't too keen on spending nearly ten thousand dollars to have a maximum body. Their literature was all about swimming with one's hips and just seemed too out there for my quick-fix needs.[3]

As I started tuning in to Gary's blog on a regular basis, I liked him more and more. He was definitely a bit of a maverick in the traditional, endurance-based swimming world. Gary had often questioned the rigid thinking represented by the various U.S. swimming organizations, often undermining their very notion of training. It wasn't until I read one of his entries, for instance, that I realized we were training all of our swimmers, from age six on up, to be endurance athletes and that this approach excluded kids who were fast-twitch athletes. "'If it isn't broken, don't fix it' doesn't work in sports. In sports we need to challenge ourselves every day to get faster. Just because the old aerobic base training for every young swimmer has taken us to where we are today in the sport doesn't make it the only or best way," he suggested in one of his calmer moments.

The typical age-group[4] program makes its swimmers practice three to four miles a day—the equivalent of

3. I end up eating those thoughts later.
4. Age-group swimming is simply a category of swimming. The other types are YMCA and Country Club. When I was a kid, age-group swimming was run by the Amateur Athletic Union and it was called AAU swimming. It later became USS (United States Swimming) and is now referred to as USA swimming.

running more than twelve miles. For a kid with a preponderance of fast-twitch fibers, this equals death or at least a one-way ticket out of the pool. Millions of potentially great young swimmers were being turned away annually simply by the style of training that dominates the sport. That was some pretty damning information and a good alternative view—just the kind of thinking I needed.

And I couldn't help but be inspired by the fact that at thirty-two years of age, Gary was one of "us" old guys. At the time I attended his camp, he hadn't announced that he was training for his fourth Olympic berth, somewhat of an Oedipal goal in that his dad, Gary Hall Sr., had competed in three Olympics. Back in 1976, when Gary Sr. was training to qualify for his third, the newspapers referred to him as the Old Man of the Sea. He was twenty-four. When he did manage to qualify, taking second place in the 100 fly at that summer's Trials, he scooped up Gary Jr., barely a toddler, and swam around the pool to the delight of the cheering crowd.

So Gary Jr. was not only older than his dad had been when he made his final Olympic bid—he was also a definite rebel. Besides railing against swimming's endurance bias, Gary had endured a short ban for testing positive for marijuana in 1998, a big no-no in this clean-cut middle America sport. Also, he liked to come out on the pool deck dressed in Everlast boxing shorts and pose like Sugar Ray Leonard. While the typical U.S. Olympic swimmer says things like, "Gee, I love Mom, apple pie, and swimming laps, not necessarily in that order," Gary hated swimming laps and would much rather be off chasing fish with a spear than training in a pool.

⌁ ⌁ ⌁

On the Overseas Highway, caught in the maddening two-lane traffic that the Keys' only thoroughfare is known for as I made my way from Miami's airport to Islamorada, home to the Race Club, I wondered just what the hell I was doing. That part of the Keys, like most of Florida, is a conservationist's nightmare, with overdevelopment and trashy tourist shop after trashy tourist shop blocking my view of what could have been some pretty cool mangrove forests. And to top things off, Cheeca Lodge, my accommodations for the week, was more of a lodge along the lines of an Econo Lodge than a fancy resort. It called itself a resort but I'm not sure what qualified it— whether it was the piped-in Jimmy Buffett tunes or simply the all-in-one, expensive pricing.

Things improved greatly, though, when Gary's sister Bebe joined us, after she picked up my fellow camper, John Fields, and his wife, Lynn. Bebe, much, much better looking than her older brother, was going to be our camp counselor for the week. So even if they did wear us down to the point of collapse, at least the last thing we'd see before passing out would be a thing of beauty.

Also, I liked the camp's mentality. Although the restaurant was only a few hundred yards across the highway, they drove us to dinner—no need to waste our important swimming muscles on walking. Waiting at the outdoor table were not only Gary Hall Jr., his wife, Elizabeth, a former model, and their newborn baby, Gigi, but also Gary Hall Sr. and his wife, Mary, whom I initially mistook for a thirty-something trophy wife. They were all dressed in white, and as a gentle breeze blew off of Florida Bay, I felt like I'd set foot on a television commercial for Pepsodent. They all looked so perfect and sparkly.

Much to my regret, during that first dinner, I didn't really get to talk with Gary Sr. very much — he was down at the far end of the table near John and Lynn, but at some point, I realized he'd done his research on us. He said something to John about Auburn, where John had swum as a walk-on during college, and later, he made a joke along the lines of "Unlike some of us, at least I'm not trying to qualify for the Olympics." I'd recently written a short piece for *Outside* magazine about my aspirations and it was a little disconcerting that he knew my ultimate goal. I wasn't ready for legitimate swimmers to know how crazy I was. Most swimmers I knew didn't read *Outside* and telling my wife, who had last competed in swimming as a ten-year-old, was one thing — telling the likes of the two Garys was another.

Even so, I went to bed with a smile on my face. Not only had Bebe laughed at the last thing I'd said and paid absolutely no attention to John, but Gary Sr., the one-time Olympic captain and U.S. Olympic squad flag bearer, was going to attend the camp with John and me.

The next morning, though, sucked.

Bebe was late picking us up because she'd stayed out

late, but that didn't matter because it was Bebe. No, what sucked was when we got to the outdoor pool and met our coaches, Jon Olsen and Andy Deichert. It's not that Jon, a laid-back, soft-spoken former Olympic champion, and Andy, a seriously cut, Fu Manchu'd all-around athlete who played football, baseball, and swam for LSU, weren't enjoyable to be around. They were. It's just that the workout was way too easy. We did half the yards I usually did on my own and nothing was hard. I'd been expecting them to kick my butt because that's what I understood it took to be great. Everyone knows that to win you have to work harder than everybody else, right? Clearly, the Race Camp didn't understand why I was in this. To them, I was just another middle-aged masters swimmer trying to beat other masters swimmers. This workout was for manatees, not the barracuda I wanted to be. All we did was stroke-work repeats, the easiest thing you can do in a workout besides warming up.

I went to a swim camp when I was twelve years old where I'd done much more than this, and another when I was a teenager where I swam eight to ten miles a day.[5] But that first morning in the Keys, we barely broke one mile.

5. Not that I want to hold up the Pinecrest School's swim camp as a shining example. They filmed us below water and then replayed the footage for all the campers to see. When I came up, the coach—this was back around 1976—said, "Hey, that's not as bad as I thought it'd be." Not really the most inspiring comment, especially since nothing else followed. And at night, one of the counselors would throw darts at unruly campers, actually connecting on many occasions. I tried to leave after the

Jon, from the pool deck, explained that to swim free-style properly, we had to flex our hips, use them to anchor our bodies to make a better rotation. "Everything you do has to have a purpose," he explained. "And it's all about anchoring your body so you can dig into that initial catch and propel yourself forward." He then did this swimmy dance thing where he flicked one hip forward while stroking freestyle through the air. Then the other side. Retrieve, flick, retrieve, flick, retrieve, flick, retrieve, flick.

Jon looked like a spasmodic Elvis, his hips rotating in near-robotic precision. This technique meant a lot to him judging by his animated expression. He reminded me of a Holy Roller suddenly touched by the Lord, and his delight was infectious. Caught up in his enthusiasm, John and I nodded in understanding.

However, I, for one, had no earthly idea what he was talking about. But I continued to listen politely and do the drills that were meant to increase our hip usage.[6]

I knew that Jon probably knew what he was talking about; he had swum in the 1992 and 1996 Olympics, collecting a total of four golds and one bronze on various relays. Relays were his forte. One U.S. Olympic team official said of Jon after his performance in the 4 × 100 free-

---

first week, but when I was told my parents wouldn't get a refund, I stuck it out for the entire, interminable three-week session.

6. I didn't know it at the time but I simply wasnt ready for it. I didn't know enough about freestyle to learn what I needed to know and I hadn't been humbled enough to rethink all that I'd taken for granted That would come much, much later, but at the time, I proceeded to get a bit depressed.

style relay at the 1996 Barcelona Olympics, "Olsen swam a monster leg. He became a man." He also swam monstrously fast in the individual 100 at the 1992 Olympics. In fact, the clock put him in third, but there was one small problem. Second through eighth looked like a tie to the naked eye and even during instant replay. That wouldn't have been a problem since there was electronic timing, but for some reason, a swimmer from Brazil hadn't received a time. The judges had to vote on who got what place to award the swimmer with no time. Just as Jon was about to walk up to the podium to receive his medal, an official pulled him back, saying the electronic timer had placed him fourth. Jon was suddenly out of a medal. A few years later one of the judges told him that, in fact, the timing system had not shown the guy who got the silver getting second, that they had simply voted it that way. Jon told this story without a trace of bitterness, but I couldn't help feeling that it dug at him, ever so slightly, despite all those gold-medal relay stints.

Andy was to be our strength and flexibility coach. With his Jeff Bridges–style ponytail, circa *The Big Lebowski,* and ready smile, he put us at ease and did a lot of talking—about what, I wasn't always sure, but he could sure talk. He sort of reminded me of one of those self-appointed orators of a New York City block—a roaming, barefoot lecturer with fire in his eyes. And he was a seriously strong cookie. His whole body seemed like it was one long, lean muscle. I'd never really seen anyone built like him. He could probably flip a sumo wrestler.

And then there was John Fields, my fellow camper. I wrote him off as a forty-nine-year-old, hulking, southern momma's boy with his pressed shirts and shorts and mild manner. All week long, I beat him in nearly every sprint and I chuckled at what a waste of time his swimming was. It seemed he couldn't get over the older-athlete mental hump to swim fast, but not all is as it seems.

"Do you really think I can do that?" he asked, his eyes growing large, reminding me more than a bit of Gomer Pyle. "I just don't think it's possible after all these years. We're just too old." All he left out was the "aw, shucks." I lectured him as much as I could, suggesting he set tougher goals.

That first afternoon, things didn't get much better, either. Instead of having another workout, we—both Garys, John, Bebe, Mary, and I—went snorkeling and spear fishing in the Race Club boat. I'd signed up for it, thinking it'd be a nice break later in the week, but now, coming so soon in our camp experience because of predicted bad weather, it just seemed like a waste of time. I wanted to get faster—not chase after grouper with a slingshot spear. I didn't catch anything and John did, in the first fifteen minutes.

In retrospect, this was a missed golden opportunity. No, not to flirt more with Bebe. I did that. But to swim really hard underwater in powerful bursts, using only my legs and holding my breath for longer and longer periods. It would have been exceptional training for sprinting and it was apparently a part of Gary Jr.'s regimen. I, however, was too narrow-minded, too results oriented, too clueless to see it for what it was. In fact, it's the kind of thing I now do at home when training for the 50—its merit having dawned on me only a few months ago.

That night, with my sensitive, sunburned skin keeping me awake, I railed against the camp. What kind of a two-bit, second-rate piece of crap was this?

"I'm sure it'll get better tomorrow, sweetie," Lisa tried, consoling me over the phone.

"No, no it won't. It's stupid. A waste of money and time."

"You're down there without a care in the world. No kids. No chores. And you're saying you can't make this work. Then come home. Get your money back," she replied. "I could really use some help. Helen put gum in Angus's hair and the twins are talking back to me. I asked them to turn off the TV and at first they didn't even . . ."

"No, no. It's not that bad here. I'll make it work," I blurted out quickly—anything was better than having to balance those four increasingly delinquent personalities. Things had gotten much better between Lisa and me, and I hazarded a guess that backpedaling would be okay. "I gotta go. There's a lizard trying to get under my covers."

The next morning, Gary Sr. joined us in the pool. He, John, and I started talking about who we knew in common as we went into the locker room to change. Those two, having been on somewhat closer playing fields, had a few common names. We started getting ready to swim and I suddenly felt awestruck. This really famous swimmer (in the swimming world, at least) was about to get in the pool with me and he was acting like one of the guys. I'm not too sure what I expected—that he was going to change in his own locker room?—but clearly it wasn't this. He was standing right next to me. Naked.

The feeling stayed with me for much of the day. I'd catch a glimpse of him out of the corner of my eye and repeat to myself, "I'm swimming with *Gary Hall*!" The younger Gary never ended up working out with us even though the camp literature said we'd be racing with the Race Club team. Since he was the only swimming member of the team currently in the area, I'd assumed he might join us, but he had a newborn at home and was still on a training hiatus. He was probably just afraid John and I would beat him.

Workout-wise, things stayed about the same in the pool. Jon swiveled his hips a lot up on the deck and taught us something he called a half-brain drill, which I would relate, but clearly, I don't even have half of one. I've forgotten it. Again, we swam very few yards compared to what I was doing back home and nearly all of it was at very little intensity. What I hadn't gotten through my head was that this was a stroke/technique camp, not a training camp. As a result, I was confused and not getting much out of it.

At least I understood the strength work. "It's all about

balance and a strong core," Andy told us during our first stint at the local gym, a place called Froggy's. He flexed his six-pack and motioned all around his torso, hips, and upper legs. "And by that, I mean you have to have a strong core. Your body is like a house. You can have all the pretty exterior work you might want but it's not going to amount to much at all, unless you have a good foundation." And then he jumped up and down like a little kid. "I'm going to show you some stuff I'm pretty excited about."

That's what I'm talking about, I thought, mentally rubbing my hands in anticipation. I was about to learn all Gary Jr.'s secrets. Everyone knew he didn't do lots of laps—so that meant, at least in my mind, that it was all about the weight room. I got prepared for some heavy lifting. However, we didn't touch a single dumbbell. Instead, we spent all our time boxing and rolling a wheel across the gym floor.

As it turned out, boxing was an integral part of Gary Jr.'s training. He is definitely fixated on the sport—with his air punching before a race, his boxer's hooded robe, and his Everlast shorts. Evidently, he also threw a lot of punches to build his core and power his hips. We learned how to box with our hips, not our arms, holding bent arms, fists closed, at chest height and twisting from side to side, landing punches on Andy's open hands. At first I found myself holding back, not wanting to hurt his hands, but he insisted that I twist harder, faster. I got the connection to Jon's hip-flexing drills but I wasn't too sure whose hands I was going to punch when I returned home. For some reason, I couldn't see Lisa yelling at me, "Harder, harder," as I pummeled the palms of her hands.

After a few rounds, I didn't feel so good. It wasn't that it tired me out because, as Andy said, I was "pretty fit." It was my ego. When John was done throwing punches, Andy had said, "Man, you've got some power!" While with me, it had only been, "Harder, harder!"

Then we turned to the wheel, an innocent-looking device that is, in fact, an insidious torture tool. It's a wee little thing — six inches in diameter — with short handles poking out of either side. Operating it was simple: you extend yourself horizontally, rolling the wheel in front of you, ending in a push-up position while holding onto the wheel. That's difficult enough, but it's the coming back that's the killer. It's all core, a catchword I was quickly learning to hate, burning as you snap back into the starting position.

Gary, John, Bebe, and I did it from our knees multiple times. We men didn't want to be outdone by a girl so we repeatedly stayed in the prone position much longer than we should have. Then somebody challenged somebody else — Gary asked Bebe, or the other way around, I forget — to do it from his/her feet. Once Bebe did it and stayed stretched out for thirty seconds, then, of course, all of us macho guys had to follow suit. Same for when she did seventy and one hundred seconds.

To my near horror, though, that's all we did in the gym that day. It was nearly impossible to master, and my body trembled like a thirteen-year-old on Ritalin, but where were the heavy bench sets, jump squats, or at least the pull-ups? No one could convince me Gary Jr. was going to win gold one more time by doing these wheelie things.

Although I was feeling like a disgruntled postal worker, I hung in there, not to see it through to the end but because I couldn't change my airline ticket. I gave in, accepting that it was a waste of time. And, of course, that's when something finally clicked. A day or so after Froggy's, before we pushed off for yet another drill, Jon said, "You use your hips to get your core to drive you forward. Flex those hips and you're going to go forward. It doesn't have to be — it shouldn't be — all shoulders." Yeah, sure. I kicked against the wall for thirty seconds like Jon had told us to do — something I hadn't done since I was three years old. Then without taking a break, I flipturned and pushed off to swim two laps while trying to retain the feel of the rotating hips from the kicking exercise. Instead of repeating, "Stroke, flex, stroke, flex," I muttered, "Stupid, hips, stupid, hips, stu —" Suddenly, I felt myself propelled forward by my . . . hips. The feeling was an epiphany.

When I got back to the wall, I looked up at Jon, and he just smiled — like I'd slipped into a place he'd been waiting for me to reach all along — and said, "You like that, huh, Hodding? Like I said, it's all about anchoring. Using your hips, your core. That kicking drill ingrains it in your head. I loved doing it at meets, but you do get some pretty weird looks."

"You can't do anything violently or suddenly in water. It even takes time for a stone to sink," William Bachrach, Johnny Weissmuller's coach, once said. "Things must be done with relaxation and undulation, like that of a snake." Although I'd used those words in a speech to my home-town Y to describe myself as a forty-three-year-old snake undulating my way to the Olympics, they hadn't really resonated. Since returning to swimming, I'd always been about blasting my way through the water. I was going to win through sheer strength and willpower. But now, thanks to Jon, I actually felt like a snake in the water: sliding through the pool with serpentine ease. Oh, except for one place—my core. Those wheel exercises I thought were such a waste had ripped nearly every muscle in my abdomen. I felt like I'd gone twelve rounds with the young Mike Tyson. But, I also realized that using Jon's hip-flexing technique required a strong, flexible core. Without Jon and Andy ever having connected them aloud, their strategies built on each other.

After that, I loved the Race Club. As John said to me over a mound of pancakes one morning, "Things are go-ing even better than I thought they would. I mean I'm in the pool swimming with a legend and learning how to go faster. What could be better than that?" The Race Club was erasing the years between our college selves and now—not by making us fitter in the pool but smarter.

Well, at least John got smarter. On the last day, when it came time to put together what we had learned, I was try-ing to think of what I'd say after I kicked his butt, seeing as how I'd been trying to build him up all week. "Better luck next time, loser," didn't seem appropriate.

As I contemplated my postrace aside, Jon said, "You two are looking good. Let's see what you've learned." We climbed up on the racing blocks and, moments later, we were flying through the air. I kept my head down and did my best to use my hips as we'd been instructed. I was feeling fast, maybe even college-level fast, when I glanced over at John beneath the water. He was ahead! I instantly notched up the tempo and flailed away in a desperate attempt to put things back in their natural order. No matter how hard I tried, though, in the end, he kicked *my* butt.[7]

I went back home a religious convert of sorts—all praise the hip!—and practiced flexing my hips day after day. I walked around the house that way, Angus following close behind, mimicking my sashaying hips. I'd thought, perhaps, that Lisa might be upset with how much time and mental focus I was devoting to swimming, but she seemed more supportive than ever. They were all going to come down to Boston to watch me swim.

---

7. Since then, we've gone to the same meets across the United States and he's proceeded to kick my behind nearly every time, all the while getting stronger and stronger. Besides trying to inspire him to faster swimming, I also spent much of that week lecturing him on how he had to focus on getting strong, that lifting weights and building strength was the only way to go as a masters athlete, and I wish I hadn't. Last I heard, he could do forty-five pull-ups in four minutes. I shudder to think how much he might bench if he put his mind to it.

At the urging of a fellow swimmer, I'd started working out with the local masters group on Saturdays and was one of their part-time coaches. It was an informal "team," and those of us who knew anything about swimming took turns leading workouts. The next time I led the workout, I found myself doing the Jon Olsen swivel dance in an attempt to win over my fellow old geezers. Most of them looked at me with the same Barney Fife expression I'd given Jon, although a few caught on.

I kept on swiveling into my taper. The New England short-course championships—my big meet for the season—were in a couple of weeks. They had filmed me at camp, and each night while Lisa was doing the dishes (at least I cooked) I'd sneak onto the computer and watch the DVD.

"Don't you think that can wait until they're all in bed," she would yell from across the house. How did she know?

I'd reflexively close the screen. "What can wait until who's in bed?" I'd yell back.

Not only did I need to flick my hips into place but I also needed them to ride higher in the water and get rid of the air bubbles that clung to my left hand. If you are pushing air bubbles underwater, then you aren't connecting with as much water as you possibly can and therefore, you are going slower than your potential. And why was I wiggling so much? *Was it too late to fix all these things before the big meet?* I thought, as I struggled with Angus's pull-up and erased the computer's recent history.

Evidently, it wasn't, although admittedly, I didn't get rid of the air bubble issue. That weekend at Harvard, armed with one of those new-fangled tech suits, I posted my best times thus far since returning. In the 200 freestyle, my premier college event, I swam five seconds faster than I did back in 2004 when I had to crawl across the pool deck at the completion of the race. I swiveled my hips for as long as I could. Still, the race was the kind in which I finished with a piano on my back. My arms filled with lactic acid by the last 50 as my need for oxygen outpaced my ability to send it where it was needed, and it took everything I had just to swing them over the top of the water. It wasn't a pretty sight, but it was fast enough to get second in my age group. Afterward, as I dried off up in the stands surrounded by my fellow Maine masters, Mike Schmidt said, "Nice race, Hodding," and I felt proud. Of course, not too proud since he'd won the race and beaten me by four-tenths of a second.

I raced the 50 and 100 freestyles over the course of the next two days and won both races for my age group, with times of 22.49 and 49.2 respectively. Not only had I swum faster than I had in twenty years, but I was now equaling my times from my sophomore year in college. Evidently, contrary to my college experience, I was better in the shorter races, and in fact, I was fifth nationwide in the 100 free for my age group, a feat I was proud of. My disdain for masters swimming had been wiped off my smirking face. I wanted to be number one.

I'd aged two years since my initial "comeback," yet I

was getting faster, not slower. If I could keep improving, I might make it to the Trials. Although I was a long, long way off—so far off that any rational person wouldn't even have perceived me as a dark horse—it seemed possible . . . at least to me.

Lisa, the kids, and I sang the whole way back home.

Four

Me and Mark Spitz

I did, however, have my own cautionary note, based mostly on personal experience. One would think I would have learned a thing or two from Mark Spitz, the former 1972 Munich Olympic great who made an ill-advised comeback attempt in his early forties. After all, I had followed his attempt rather closely. Back in 1990, as a desperate twenty-seven-year-old writer, I pitched a story about Mark to *Esquire* so I could swim my way out of my position at the magazine: fact-checker. Being a fact-checker had seemed sort of glamorous in the wake of Jay McInerney's 1980s-writer-generation-defining novel *Bright Lights, Big City,* but in reality, it sucked. Something about checking whether or not Paul Newman had real teeth instead of dentures or that Michael Dukakis wore shoe polish in his hair didn't seem to represent Successful Writer to me. I wanted to be writing those things — not finding out if they were correct or not. So, when I heard my childhood hero, Mark Spitz, was making a comeback, I was all over the story—sneaking into the editors' offices and sticking Post-its scrawled with my knowledge of and prowess in swimming all over the place. Evidently, they had no choice but to buckle under my assault, and a few weeks later, I found myself flying out to L.A. *on assignment* for a national magazine.

I wanted to drink a dozen shots of mezcal, I was so excited. (Real writers are alcoholics, right?) There I was, willing to write about anything to get my name in print and had even pitched a story along those lines: "Your Belly Button—The Inside Story." Instead, I was writing about my favorite sport and my childhood hero and reporting it from L.A. Obviously, there'd been some kind of mistake. Who gets to hang out with his hero and have an expense account for the first time in his life *at the same time?* It was an Olympic, dreamy opportunity. So what was I doing writing things like this just a few weeks later: "I began to smell chlorine everywhere. I checked myself first, sniffing under my arms. It wasn't coming from me. Mark probably didn't notice but a Chlorine Effect Aura (CEA) began to encircle him. The more he spoke about his swimming future, the stronger the CEA grew. When it came out that he might be going for at least four medals in Barcelona, I could barely see him through the acrid haze that had risen between us."

I employed those words and even more damning ones in my story that was published in *Esquire* in the May 1990 issue. Mark's father-in-law was in charge of his PR and he had Mark on a fairly short leash, given Mark's age. Mark had a bit of the motor-mouth in his younger years and Herman didn't want a repetition of zingers like, "Maybe I'll do some nudie movies. I'm hot to trot. Yeah, maybe I'll do a little trotting before we make the movie." Apparently, Mark had been, in Herman's words, "a prick" and such quotes were more the norm than not. While kids like me in 1972 ended up worshipping his life-size poster—the one with Mark in his red, white, and blue swimsuit and all seven record-setting glittering gold Olympic medals strung around his broad, hairy chest—older people (like my editor at *Esquire*, David Hershey, but more on that in a minute) apparently hated him for his arrogance and obnoxious chatter. So Mark's father-in-law originally granted me only one interview and one swim.

I'd trained furiously in the few weeks that I had between the assignment and our actual get-together. It wasn't just that I wanted to keep up with him for the sake of the story—after all, I'd told my editor that I was a great swimmer—but I also wanted Mark to notice that I had the right stuff.

He didn't. He said hello. Yawned. Stretched. Told me that Rod Stewart was short and annoying. Undressed. The coach, who looked both bewildered and bemused with having to deal with me, stuck us in the same lane, at the end of the pool with the sprinters. And then Mark and I dutifully started our workout. I'm not sure what I was expecting beyond a golden ray arcing through the sky, trumpets blaring, embracing us in a heavenly spotlight, but it didn't happen. I noticed things, though. His black hair was now speckled with white and that taut belly of yesteryear looked pretty much like any other thirty-nine-year-old's (his age at the time; he'd be forty-two once the Olympics arrived). He was puffy. In fact, he reminded me of my dad when he was forty. My dad didn't look bad for his age. In fact, people always commented on how young my dad looked, but he didn't look, well, Herculean. Mark, like my dad, definitely didn't look like he could kick some twenty-year-old's butt.

Although I had my blinders on, even I couldn't help wondering how in the name of hell he was going to do it. Yes, he'd been the greatest swimmer ever, but clearly, that was no longer the case. I, the wiggly tadpole in comparison, was keeping up with him. I quickly squashed those thoughts, suppressed them like the memories of me running naked through my neighbor's yard and said neighbor's mother scolding me with, "We don't do that kind of thing around here, young man." I finished the swim, interviewed him the next day, and even went boating with him the day after, once Herman decided I wasn't going to destroy Mark in print.

I returned to New York and wrote a very hopeful, sweet piece about hanging out with my childhood hero: "The Munich Kid will rise again and all will be right with the world." It was good, heartfelt stuff—the kind of story Horatio Alger would have been proud of.

"Bullshit," David, my dashing, Hollywood-handsome editor,[1] bellowed when I anxiously answered the summons to his office. "No way this is going in the magazine, Hodding. That's not the Mark Spitz I remember. He's an asshole. Everybody knows that. Do you really think he's going to make it?"

"Um, no."

"Then why'd you write he would? Listen, this guy was an ass in '72 and I'm sure he still is now. I'll give you one more chance, but hit him hard or . . ." There was no need to finish the sentence. I knew the "or else." Or else I'd be making calls like, "Is it true that Joe really picked up his newspaper with a pair of pliers?" to Joe's next-door neighbor from 1981 for the rest of my miserable failed-writer's life. And there was no way that was going to happen.

The one thing I wanted, even more than I'd ever wanted to make it to the Olympics, was to make it as a writer. My grandfather had been a Pulitzer Prize–winning journalist in Mississippi in the middle of the last century, bravely calling for equal opportunity for blacks in daily editorials even though he'd been raised a racist. He'd also authored some seventeen nonfiction books and won uncountable awards doing so. My own father had lived under this shadow but managed to carve out a nice writing niche for

1. He wouldn't let me use this quote unless I described him thusly—although I'd rather suggest he's more like a good-looking Geraldo Rivera.

himself, whipping out delightful, award-winning tirades against the Reagan administration for the *Wall Street Journal*. The day I announced I wanted to be a writer, both my dad and my grandmother (my grandfather died in 1972) all but laughed aloud and suggested I might try another profession, perhaps teaching. The thought of my becoming a writer seemed ludicrous to them and so from that day forth it was all I desired. My entire existence relied on my becoming not only a writer but a writer that would somehow or another outshine my predecessors.

Mark Spitz was my magic carpet and there was no way I was falling off that ride.

Unsurprisingly, within twenty-four hours, I suddenly had a completely different interpretation of Mark's comeback. Where I had been deferential, I was now snide. Harsh reality chased Pollyanna right out of the pool. Here's an excerpt of what eventually ran in the magazine (the article was entitled, "The Further Wet Dreams of Mark Spitz"; this was probably the most damning thing in the piece):

> Mark tried to explain, "Instead of being a should've, a could've, I *am*. It's a challenge out there to do. . . . I would hate not having gotten off my rear end and tried."
>
> Mark Spitz, who set twenty-eight world records and appeared on the front page of the *New York Times* three times within five days, "a

should've, a could've"? One of us had gotten too much water in his ear.

He continued talking, describing his new, media-conscious self. "This time around I got together with a friend to put an angle on the story, tell it properly," he said. "Back then, we weren't as well polished and versed in PR."

I began to worry. Could Mark be suffering from the dread Chlorine Effect, a little-known malady that typically robs middle-aged men of their hard-won maturity?

I called Don Schollander, a four-time gold medal winner at the '64 Olympics and a teammate of Spitz's in '68. In the past, Schollander appeared to understand Spitz the best. I asked Schollander how he felt about Spitz's "biggest fear"—that other swimmers might come out of retirement as well. Schollander, forty-three, laughed heartily.

"Tell Mark I'll challenge him at the earliest time possible," he said, still laughing. "No, no, really. I've already had my midlife crisis."

"Do you think Spitz will make the Olympic team?" I asked.

"No, I don't," Schollander said. "I think he should sit down and think about it long and hard. Mark always had a certain blind confidence. I think he still has it. But now it may be blinding *him*."

. . . At a pool somewhere in California, Mark whiffed in a heavy cloud of chlorine. His reasoning faltered and, weakened, Mark began talking about putting on the old red, white, and blue swimming suit one more time. Herman and Suzy, Mark's wife, thought it was ridiculous, but they were too late. The Chlorine Effect had nabbed another victim.

"I know what I want to do," Mark told me, "but I can't tell you. If I can do it, it will be mind-boggling."

"What can you tell me?" I asked.

"Well . . . my goal is to set the world record in the 100 fly." At that time the world record was two seconds faster than his 1972 standard, and that's in a race in which a tenth of a second is a vast improvement. By the time you read this, some seventeen-year-old will have dropped it another couple of tenths.

"Well, what new technology are you going to use?" I asked. "Lactate testing, Swim Bench, buckets?"

"None. I don't believe in that stuff," he huffed.

I began to smell chlorine everywhere. I checked myself first, sniffing under my arms. It wasn't coming from me.

Mark probably didn't notice but a Chlorine Effect Aura (CEA) began to encircle him. The more he spoke about his swimming future, the stronger the CEA grew. When it came out that he might be going for at least four medals in Barcelona, I could barely see him through the acrid haze that had risen between us.

As Mark continued to explain himself, my thoughts drifted back to our workout in the UCLA pool. He had looked good in the water *for a thirty-nine-year-old.* The water didn't slide off of him as much as it rolled around his body, searching for holes and pockets to fill—treating him much like the ocean does an old junk on its last opium run. While the younger swimmers in his lane completed more than 3.5 miles, he managed only 2.5. Mark even escaped to the bathroom twice during a difficult set. All in all, he resembled certain guys I swam with in college—a little overweight and lazy, but talented.

I had trained nearly six weeks in preparation for our encounter, beginning the very day I heard Spitz was back in the water. I had also reread *Heroes of the Olympics,* paying particular attention to the final passage: "It isn't more skill or physical strength that wins Olympic victories. But it is the desire to use that talent, sometimes in the face of great odds, that makes heroes of the Olympics."

That's why I had thought Mark Spitz would be the very first forty-two-year-old ever to swim to a gold medal in the Olympics. He had that magical combination. I've always believed in that passage . . . and still do. That's how I knew, when I first heard that he was attempting a comeback, Spitz would win again, and good (desire in a worthy heart) would triumph over evil (great odds).

But then, standing on the pool deck with an all-too-meaningful sun setting over the Pacific Ocean, I watched my childhood hero slack off, skipping laps during a long-distance set.

A few minutes later his coach, who had not been watching, walked over to his lane and asked everyone if they'd completed the entire swim. Mark glanced up, his dark goggles shielding his eyes. I caught my breath, hoping this thirty-nine-year-old man would say, "Oh, you know. I'm just taking it easy, doing what I can. I didn't finish it all but don't worry. It'll come." Then I'd return home and tell my friends all was right in the world, that 1992 would be the year of a true Olympic Hero. But Mark had his own world to live in. Did he swim the entire set? His answer, "Yep."

The magazine received a handful of complimentary letters on the article, along with one or two particularly knowledgeable, vitriolic attacks against me for writing the story. One of the letters referred to me as Hod, a nickname that I'd told Herman to call me, and was filled with information about Mark that mostly only someone close to him would know. I was sure the letter had been written by Herman, and it hurt me to no end because he suggested I'd written such a harsh story so I could get published. That I had sold out. How had he known?

I've regretted that article ever since it left my typewriter (we were still using them back then). It gave me a good clipping for my portfolio and set me on my writing career, but in some way, that article has also tainted it, like I got here on Mark's bloodied back. People who know him have since told me that I was dead-on, but even so, I still wish I hadn't given in. Not because I was wrong. I think I was probably right. Spitz probably was attempting a comeback because he might be able to get some sponsorship money or land a sweet speaking engagement or two. He kept swimming for another year or so. His name started popping up in the press more frequently. He got one of the networks to pay him to race against Matt Biondi, America's fastest butterflier at the time, and air the duels in the pool, but he never came close to his old best time in the 100 fly or even the Olympic Trials qualifying time, which was two seconds slower. It seemed like he was just in it for the money.

Now, a much wiser forty-five-year-old with the same desperate but less likely goal of making it to the Olympics, I have to ask myself, "So what?" He was one of the greatest swimmers ever and the winningest Olympian in history. His record is still unbroken—seven gold medals in one Olympics. It's astounding. Yet there he was daring to put all that aside and attempting to trump it before millions of people. He deserved a second chance at all that money corporate America throws at our successful athletes. Who was I to condemn him? Yes, he'd made a whopping $7 million right after the Olympics, an unimaginable sum for an athlete back in the early seventies, but clearly he needed more. Given that I would do just about anything to get out from under my own seemingly insurmountable personal debt, I certainly wouldn't begrudge him for trying such a novel and unflinching strategy.

And what if I was wrong? What if doing it for the money was his beard, so to speak—his cover to keep his wife and father-in-law in the dark. Doing it for the money was the kind of reason they and everybody else would understand. It might make some desperate hack like me take potshots at him, but generally it would deflect the public's laughter and his family's dismay. Any adult would understand another adult doing something screwy for money. But what if his real reason was because he truly thought he could make it and he didn't want to grow old not having tried—not having laid it all on the line to become the oldest man ever to swim at the Olympics, or even the Olympic Trials for that matter? What if deep in his soul he knew that if he didn't give it one more chance, he'd regret it every single day, every single time he looked in the mirror, for the rest of his probably long life, given all the exercise he'd had over the years? If that was the case, then I have to say just one thing to Mark Spitz.

I'm sorry.

Five

Like a Different Species?

These days, Mark's comeback attempt doesn't seem so silly—at least not to me.

Seriously, though, even before I started training, my expectations for what happens to people as they age had changed. I no longer think, as Don Schollander once did, "And then I turned forty." Today, forty-and-older athletes beating competitors in their thirties, twenties, and teens is almost commonplace. There appears to have been some sort of colossal breakthrough for older athletes. Baseball alone can field an entire team of over-forty all-star players including Roger Clemens, Barry Bonds, Randy Johnson, and Moises Alou, to name just a few (not all of them were on steroids).

Even so, initially, practically everybody laughed at the absurdity of my quest—not just because it was me but because of my age. Jim Steen, my college coach and winner of twenty-eight consecutive national titles, said, "Well, Hoddo, your timing always was a bit off."

Not too soon after I returned to swimming, a friend of mine told a dinner party of a dozen friends about my goal and there was an immediate, nearly unanimous guffaw. They weren't laughing because they knew me, but because they all knew that an athlete in his forties did not stand a chance against a younger athlete. Swimming was a sport for juveniles, not someone on the shortlist for a pair of Depends. That was a fact, based not only on common sense but apparently irrefutable evidence.

For starters, there was the iron-clad 1 percent rule. According to this well-known rule, we decline by 1 percent in our ability to perform physiological feats and functions after the age of twenty-five, including dropping 1 percent of muscle mass every year. For instance, the biceps of a newborn baby have roughly 500,000 fibers while those of your average eighty-year-old have only 300,000.

The older athlete simply didn't stand a chance. We weren't as strong. Our ability to uptake oxygen decreased. Our reaction times were slower. We couldn't recover enough to work out hard enough to be competitive. Our hearts couldn't beat as fast as a younger person's. Our body-fat percentage increased no matter what we did, creating that inevitable girth that accompanies middle age. Not only was it crazy to aim for the Olympics, it was moronic to hope for more than merely slouching into the Centrum Silver years.

Such common wisdom, however, was totally mistaken.

I didn't start out knowing this. In fact, I believed and expected everybody over forty, except for me, to look more like Gollum than the Hulk. So I took it in stride when people chuckled whenever I mentioned my goal, and when I initially failed to swim as fast as I thought I could, I decided I needed some proof that it was possible. If I couldn't immediately prove to people that they were wrong, maybe I could find a talking head to do it for me.

That's when I happened upon Joel Stager, director of Indiana University's Counsilman Center for the Science of Swimming and a noted kinesiologist. Although we've never met, these days I think of him as my guide through the trampling throngs of naysayers. Whenever I was doubted, I reread his e-mails or looked up one of his studies on the Internet. Why? He and his team of researchers have trounced our hard-held notions of aging and paved the way for people like me to follow.

"You know that stuff about losing 1 percent a year after your twenties? Baloney. If you stimulate muscle, it still responds even into your eighties. So whatever you do, Hodding, don't listen to convention," he warned me one day after I told him I thought I was too old after a particularly dispiriting workout. Luckily, Joel, besides being an expert on aging swimmers with exhaustive studies to back up his claims, is himself an outstanding, record-setting masters swimmer. He wasn't just speaking from behind thick glasses but was in the pool, proving the theories himself. "You don't have to conform if you maintain your activity level."

Other researchers have made it clear that what we think of as aging is actually just the by-product of sedentary lifestyles. "'Use it or lose it' is the guiding principal here," Phillip Whitten, a Harvard-educated gerontologist, wrote in *Swimming World* magazine in March 2005, "and the sad fact of the matter is that most Americans simply don't use it." If you work out, he claimed, you can attain or retain the strength and vitality of your youth. If you don't, you won't.

This isn't to say that I could find anyone claiming that we don't age. Some things, at least for now, do happen to all of us, unless you happen to have a lot of money. Everybody's skin gets thinner and less elastic and thus wrinkly and more susceptible to damage. Your bones become more visible because less fat gets stored just beneath your skin. And your memory generally gets worse. Then, when you get really old, say one hundred, for instance, and you're one of those people they're interviewing on the *Today* show, your veins give out on you and you eventually die.

As of right now, nearly all of those things are going to happen to us no matter what we do or how well we take care of ourselves, although it's probably not that far away when science will figure out how to stave off some of those conditions as well.[1] It wasn't that long ago that we all knew that bones become more brittle as we age thanks to their growing inability to retain calcium. It was irrefut-

---

1. A friend of mine has a plan to live to two hundred, and there are certain institutes spending tens of millions of dollars a year attempting to figure out how this might be possible.

able—except we now all know that if you eat a diet rich in calcium and, perhaps more importantly, lift weights, you can have strong, healthy bones well into your golden years and beyond. There was, for example, the gorgeous, blond Swedish bodybuilder Eva Birath: at the age of forty-seven, she was laid off from her job as a marketing executive and, to pass her newly acquired free time, she started going to the gym. Four and a half years later—at the age of fifty-one—she took third place at the Swedish national championships, leaving women half her age in her substantial wake. Her bones are very, very strong.

Putting it simply, we just don't age like we used to, and athletes are no exception.

I'd like to put myself up as case study number one, except as of this moment, since I still haven't qualified for the Olympic Trials, I'll hold off (although, of course, by the time you read this book, I will have—fingers crossed). Practically every week, however, headlines from national magazines and newspapers scream out far better examples, the most obvious one within the swimming world being Dara Torres, the current sprint phenom who set the American record in the 50 freestyle this past summer at the age of forty. Torres, a tall (six foot one), strong, beautiful woman, has had her ups and downs just like the rest of us, but in my mind her ups have far outweighed her downs. She has raced in four Olympics (now qualified in five Olympic Trials), won gold on numerous occasions, and looks more than likely to be a medal winner one more time at the age of forty-one.

Torres, who vowed never to return to race in swimming after the 2000 Olympics, began swimming again in 2005, after learning she was pregnant. Her doctor had suggested it as a low-impact way to stay in shape during her pregnancy. As her stomach grew bigger, oddly, so did her desire to compete yet again. She started talking about the 2008 Olympics, and with her eye on Beijing, she lifted weights and swam the same day she gave birth to her daughter, Tessa Grace, in April 2006. Then, in the summer of 2007, just sixteen months after Tessa's birth, Torres won both the 50 and 100 freestyles at the USA National Championships.

As you might expect, she was an insta-celebrity. She made all the talk shows, including *Charlie Rose*, and ABC News crowned her Person of the Week. Not only was everybody praising Torres, but they were also treating her like she was some sort of miracle. Her coach, Michael Lohberg, said, "Her comeback is mind-boggling. I don't think people can actually comprehend what is happening here. It hasn't happened before and probably won't happen again. A forty-year-old who hasn't been swimming for years should never go this fast." Her training partner, Leila Vaziri, the world-record holder in the fifty meter backstroke, added, "She's like a different species."

But was she really? And was Coach Lohberg correct that we probably will never see this happen again?

Once again, I turned to Joel, who responded, "Our data on the average age of the most successful swimmers continues to suggest that that age is increasing and will likely continue to do so! Dara is evidence of that. We see it in marathons, baseball, soccer, etc. Why shouldn't we see it in swimming?"[2]

"I don't think Dara is an anomaly," Joel added, "except for the fact that she continues to be motivated, has the opportunity to train and compete, and apparently has adequate incentive to do so. She has broken through the barrier and hopefully will be the example that other great swimmers will follow."

Joel has done studies showing that an athlete needs three things to be successful: motivation, opportunity, and incentive. As he pointed out, Torres has all three.

But was that all it took?

Trying to convince my wife, friends, parents, and anybody else who had heard of my goal that I hadn't completely gone off the deep end, I talked to other sports physiologists as well, like Greg Payne, chairman of the Kinesiology Department at San Jose State University, who added one more ingredient to Joel's must-haves for the older athlete to succeed: brainwashing detox.

"You have to overcome very difficult sociological factors that are working against you, which very quickly become psychological," he told me. In other words, for our whole

---

2. Interestingly, the same is also true in other areas of human endeavor as well. The average age of great intellectual achievement has increased by five to six years over the last century, according to a study that looked at Nobel Prize winners in physics, chemistry, medicine, and economics. So, not only are we getting stronger as we get older, we're also getting smarter.

lives we've been told that aging means getting slower, losing muscle, doing sports only to fight off the inevitable paunch. We are conditioned by society to "know" that we can run fast only when we're young. Overcoming that mindset is, perhaps, the major battle. "You simply can't help but be affected by those prevailing negative comments asserting that when you get older, you get slower."

And so I didn't tell my fellow masters swimmers I was training for the Olympics. I didn't want them to laugh at me. They would laugh not only because my times were so far off from qualifying times but also because they had all bought into the notion that they couldn't reclaim their former glory. And maybe they couldn't. To try and compete with younger people as an adult takes all of those things that Joel and Greg stated plus one more crucial ingredient: time. And to have time quite often means — at least once you've graduated from college — to have no life, or lots and lots of money, or as in my current case, the perfect job.

The few masters swimmers to whom I mentioned my goal either ribbed me every time they saw me — "How's the quest going, Don Quixote?" one asked — or laughed conspiratorially when I first brought it up. Those that laughed had the same idea when they first returned to swimming. Some of the people I've admitted my goal to have responded by relating similar goals and ensuing painful experiences. The difference between many of them and me, however, was that most of them decided it was a momentary brain fart — that it was impossible for somebody in their forties to do as well as he/she did in his/her late teens or twenties. I played along, laughed with them, and acted like I, too, had given up on that silly notion.

Mike Schmidt, a former NCAA Division II national champion and current guru on the science of swimming for those of us in New England, epitomized the prevailing wisdom on this subject: he thought it was nuts to think he could swim as fast as he once did. I recently misremembered that he was one of those people who believed he could still match this old times, and he bristled at the suggestion—not the reaction I wanted since his physique was more akin to the Incredible Hulk than the proverbial swimmer's body. Luckily, the bristle was via e-mail. "Your memory is playing tricks on you," he wrote. "I told you the opposite . . . having been a distance swimmer I never thought this was realistic. First, I couldn't train the way I did, and second, even if I had the time to train as much as I did in college, my body wouldn't tolerate the training. So in the absence of magic fairy dust, I never thought this possible."[3]

I found myself feeling chastised. The area where older swimmers of superior ability have beaten younger athletes

3. Mike and I are the same age and as you might be able to tell from this exchange, a bit apprehensive of each other since we're the two fastest currently active masters freestylers in Maine. We have conveniently staked out different ends of the racing range—he does distance, I do sprints—but there are moments and places of overlap. Thank God. Once I've swum at the Olympics, he'll be the main thing that keeps me going. I can't stand the idea of his beating me at the 200 free, which he currently does.

is generally in the shorter events — those that require perfect technique coupled with power and/or strength. As I've pointed out, we can hold onto or increase strength and therefore power, and given that we've been doing the activity much longer, we have the potential for having better technique. But, in those events that tax our aerobic threshold, we stand less of a chance simply because we can't afford the lifestyle that training for longer events would demand. I had four kids and a wife who worked full-time; I couldn't — without expecting to be served with divorce papers — swim four to five hours a day, lift weights or do yoga for another hour and a half, and spend two hours eating.

Yet, again, after I stepped back from conventional thinking, I realized that I was buying into the wrong notion. Some of the world's greatest runners of the marathon — the endurance race of endurance races — found the time to train many hours a day, and quite a few of them are what was once considered to be over-the-hill. Also, studies have shown that endurance athletes not only can increase slow-twitch fibers — the mainstay of distance competitions — by as much as 20 percent as they age, but they also can maintain almost all of their aerobic capacity into their fifties. And Joel Stager had gigabytes and gigabytes of statistics of older swimmers excelling at distance races. By excelling, I mean these swimmers, who were high-caliber swimmers in their youth, were beating or nearly equaling their times from twenty to thirty years back.

They were not, however, qualifying for the Olympic Trials, but I attributed that failure to two key points. One was being older and wiser. Racing and training for the 800- or 1,500-meter freestyle is infinitely more grueling and exhausting than training for the 50, 100, or 200 freestyles, races that are over in a matter of seconds. The other factor was lowered expectations brought on by cultural conditioning, the effect discussed earlier.

Although Mike initially did not hope for fast times when racing, that old nagging feeling crept up on him and he found himself wishing for them anyway. "For two cycles I didn't do as well as I hoped, which led me to see expectations only served to take the fun out of swimming," he explained in his very precise language. Mike is currently a stay-at-home dad who used to be a stressed out lawyer. Like many lawyers, he knows how easily people misunderstand each other and he is careful with his words, especially since I record every one of his. "So I worked on getting rid of expectations. After that I've always been happy to be right where my times were."

And I wished he wasn't. I watched him swim, jealously noticed his powerful build, and I knew that with the proper training, he could still be a championship distance swimmer. Like most of us, he didn't have the right income or lifestyle to make this possible (Dara Torres, from what I understand, is loaded) and perhaps he was content with what he did, but I thought he and everybody else had been duped into thinking, *I'm in my forties, I can't possibly beat my younger self, I have grown-up responsibilities,* etc.

Also, he and all the rest were clearly not going through a midlife crisis.[4]

There were more and more swimmers who were beginning to come to their senses, though. While she had received the most publicity, Dara Torres was far from being the only senior citizen in contention for some very fresh Peking duck. Half a dozen women over thirty have qualified for the Olympic Trials, including the forty-two-year-old Susan von der Lippe. She'll be forty-three by the time the Trials roll around in early summer 2008 and has a chance of making the team as a 100-yard breaststroker. Even if she doesn't make the Olympic team,[5] she'll be the second oldest swimmer ever to qualify for the Olympic swimming Trials. (The oldest? Me, of course.)

---

4. Mike had had his own crisis about fifteen years ago, when he was suddenly struck with aplastic anemia, a life-threatening condition where a person's bone marrow stops doing its job producing blood. Immediately, his life depended on getting daily blood transfusions, and if not for a lucky bone marrow transplant a few months later (odds of finding an unrelated donor—none of his relatives' blood antigen matched—are something like a million to one), he'd still be hooked to a gurney today.

5. The women's and men's teams are allowed to field twenty-six swimmers each to compete in the fourteen Olympic events. The top finisher in each event at the Olympic Trials automatically qualifies for the U.S. Olympic team, except in the 100 freestyle and the 200, where the top four finishers are selected. Those events get the extra swimmers because of the 400 and 800 freestyle relays. After that, the second-place finisher in each event is chosen until the maximum number of swimmers is reached.

On the other side of the spectrum, quite a few men over thirty have held up their end of things as well. In the years preceding the last Olympics, Paul Carter fought hard to become the oldest man ever to qualify for the Olympic Trials and/or go to the Olympics. In the summer before the Olympics, at the age of forty-five, he was less than a second off qualifying for the Trials. Currently, Gary Hall Jr., thirty-three, not only has qualified for the Trials, but is in serious contention for an Olympic Village bunk bed. He won the 50 freestyle in the last Olympics at twenty-nine and could lay claim to the title of the world's second fastest swimmer ever.[6] My money is on him for 2008.

Why are all these "old guys" doing so well? When you stop to think about Joel Stager's trilogy—motivation, opportunity, and incentive—all three have changed in the past thirty years. People are more motivated to compete as they did when they were younger for one dominating reason. They want to be young, and I am, sadly, no exception. All I had to do was turn on my television, or go to YouTube, and it was clear that the youth had usurped our culture. If I wanted to be on top, I had to appear young. Take a look at your local plastic surgeon's home; I bet it's a whole lot nicer than yours.

So let's assume we, as a culture, are all motivated to appear young. One of the many ways in which we can do

6. The 50 is akin in effort and racing time to the 200-meter running sprint but as far as bragging rights go, it's more like the 100-meter dash. It's swimming's shortest event and its competitors are the fastest swimmers, the sprint kings of the aquatic realm.

this is by competing against and beating our underlings. If you can get your heart to beat like a typical twenty-year-old's, hit the ball farther than the latest recruit, or show a bicep that'd make Arnold quiver, then you appear young. If you appear young, you get the job, win the hot lover, or are invited to the in couple's Fourth of July party. There's your motivation, and it's a hell of a lot cheaper than plastic surgery.

As far as opportunity goes, I couldn't imagine my father or mother spending two hours a day working out, five to six days a week; they would have been chased out of town in the back of a Ford Pinto. Most masters athletics had not even been initiated when I was a kid and certainly not in Mississippi. There was nowhere for them to get serious about competing. Had my mom showed up at morning swim practice or trotted out to left field to catch fly balls during Little League practice, I would've been the laughingstock of the team. Also, beyond a daily jog, there wasn't time in the day for such antics. Often these days employers will not only pay employees to work out but also provide the facility for doing so. What would have one time been frowned upon—working out during the work day—is now actively encouraged. In fact, it's almost a requirement.

And then there's the matter of incentive. In the past, only a few sports had professional leagues. There were no professional opportunities for running, competing in triathlons, or skateboarding, for instance, and for women, there was no professional anything beyond tennis and golf (and a short-lived baseball league). These days, however, if there's a sport, then there's a way to make money doing it. In other words, I could make money by swimming! And I could make it in more ways than one. The merchandising and advertising Worlds had matured (so to speak) tremendously since my parents were my age, and even swimmers, those athletes that the American public remembers only once every four years, now were making millions through endorsements, advertising, and speaking. Since the outrageous was now the commonplace in American society, swimmers could make money in ways that would have been tantamount to expulsion from USA Swimming not very many years ago. Amanda Beard, the dark-haired beauty who won three medals at the 2004 Athens Olympics, has a contract with Speedo and supplemented that income in the summer of 2007 by posing in *Playboy*.[7] Not that I'm suggesting that I had a shot at a centerfold, but imagine the Viagra and Preparation H contracts I might land. Talk about incentive!

Thanks to Joel Stager and his fellow sports scientists and the cadre of successful older athletes, I soon realized after returning to swimming that what I desired — making it to the Olympics at forty-five — was theoretically possible. Only one question remained: Was I the right man for the job?

---

7. My wife has told me that buying that issue would not count as research.

Six

SwimTrekking

It was a scorcher of an afternoon down on the sandy cove at the Little Dix Bay Lodge in Virgin Gorda. The kind of afternoon that makes babies cry and women lust for a different life, and certainly a different husband.

Two lean men kitted out in sleek Speedos swam around the point pulling behind them a surfboard loaded with gear. Unlike everyone on shore, they were cool, efficient, set in their actions. In a matter of seconds, they'd swum to shore, peeled off their goggles, hidden their craft, and changed into casual beachwear. A speedboat loaded with evil henchmen shouldering automatic rifles sped by, never the wiser of their location.

A hot mama in a tight black bikini pulled down her shades and inquired, "Where'd you two come from?" Her eyes devoured them from head to toe.

Thinking it wise not to divulge everything, the darker-haired one of the duo said they'd just swum from the ferry landing.

"Wow," she said, "that's so cool."

Meanwhile, a beach waitress stopped by, asking them for their order.

"Martini. Shaken, not stirred."

"Your name?"

"Carter . . . Hodding Carter."

Duhn-nuh, nuh, nuh-na, Duhn-na, nuh, nuh-na, Duhn, nah, nuh, nuh-na — nuh-nah![1]

✪ ✪ ✪

It's a lot harder than you might think to swim from island to island across four-knot currents, gargling salt-water hour after hour, possibly getting chased by sharks, and towing your worldly possessions on a five-foot surf-board while flying the British flag. (It's even harder when you're told on your very first day in the British Virgin Islands that your British naval flag is actually a Swiss flag.) Your mind plays tricks on you. What with the jellyfish, hecklers, and excessive rum intake, you might even think twice about swimming your way through the Caribbean. But that was my next big swim after New England.

Back when I was a Peace Corps volunteer after college, during my second year in Kenya, I started running, at seven-thousand-foot elevation. I'd probably run a total of twenty miles my entire life up to that point, but it was the only way I could get my heart and lungs back into

1. It's the James Bond theme song.

shape. I'd decided that I was going to try to qualify for the Olympics when I got home. So I endured day after day of local schoolchildren mocking me as I ran by their houses and huts, chasing after and past me, tailing me for miles, all the while yelling out, *"Mzungu, mzungu, mzungu."* It literally meant "white man, white man, white man," but depending on how it was uttered could also be translated as "scary white man," "decent white man," "stupid white man," or "crazy white man." In this case, it was invariably the last translation that was meant. They laughed even harder when I would go into my backyard and do sets of bench presses with my homemade weights. Their laughter hurt even more then because I was particularly proud of these weights, having never worked with cement before. To make the weights, which ended up looking like the tires on Fred Flintstone's car, I'd poured concrete into circles I'd dug in the ground and used tubes from toilet paper rolls to make holes in the middle of the circles. I had a set of six weights of three different sizes. Having lifted in college for swimming, I guessed the grand total, including the bar, to be about two hundred pounds—more than enough for me to train with. Anyway, when I would lift my homemade weights in my backyard, my neighbors would howl with laughter, often falling on the ground doing so, yelling out for their friends to come watch, too. While I may not have done much good when volunteering in Africa, I certainly provided some good entertainment.

As I lifted and ran, I daydreamed about my future swimming career. By this point in my life, I was no longer swayed by television coverage of well-nourished Americans defeating people from lesser-advantaged countries. I didn't want to swim simply to make it to the Olympics and win medals. In fact, I looked on this part of swimming as just another jingoistic American activity—yet another place where America flaunted its dominance. No, I no longer wanted to be at the Olympics to win gold but instead wanted to swim at the Olympics and win so I could then swim as a career to finance my writing. I knew I wouldn't make any money writing, and I figured the best way to finance the nasty habit would be by swimming. I'd swim at the Olympics and win. Afterward, I would become a millionaire through endorsements. Once I did that, I could sit back and write whatever I wanted. From there onward, whenever I needed money, I could do some kind of high-stakes match race on television or, better yet, get chosen by ABC to compete in its competition show, *Superstars*.[2] Like Johnny Weissmuller playing Tarzan for the movies, I was going to live off my swimming.

It never happened—until now. I'd pitched a story to *Outside* magazine about swimming from island to island in the Caribbean, staying at swanky resorts along the

---

2. I liked watching that show as much as I liked watching swimming. Back then, swimming was on TV about once or twice a year, unless it was the Olympics. During the *Superstars* reign, swimming, being one of the ten events in the competition, was thrust into the limelight week after week. How could I not love it? And, better yet, I stood a good chance at winning since I was absolutely the best at obstacle courses and loved tennis. What professional football player stood a chance against me?

way—sort of like trekking across France on a bike—and oddly enough, they went for it. Lisa was all for it because . . . well, because she's the sweetest person in the world when it comes to me and because we weren't paying for my trip. The magazine was.

Originally, I settled on swimming in the Grenadines in the Windward Islands because there were so many of them, and they seemed more exotic than most Caribbean islands. When I wrote to a sailing captain about my plans, however, he said that they were close enough together if I was a strong swimmer, but what about the sharks? Having an inexplicable fear of those cute little predators, I then chose the British Virgin Islands because they looked close to one another on a Web site's cartoon map and because when I mentioned them to a group of sailors who'd been down there many times, none of them mentioned sharks.

The southeast trade winds dictated a westerly route: Virgin Gorda, Ginger, Cooper, Peter, and Norman. Ginger Island was uninhabited, so I'd have to camp, but the rest was resort splendor all the way. Twenty miles of fun-filled Caribbean waters, if you could put out of your mind what the St. John–based kayak guide told me.

"Oh. Ginger, huh?" Arawak Expeditions owner Arthur Jones said when he heard my plan. "I don't know—it's pretty sharky. I remember hearing about someone else who tried that off St. John a while back, and she had to stop halfway through because of a shark. It just started following her and getting closer and closer. But I don't know. Maybe that was just a rumor."

This was after *Outside* had bought the plane ticket and after the really expensive dinner Lisa, the kids, and I had in celebration of my swimming paying for itself. In other words, I had to go. Suddenly remembering that old bear joke—the one about not having to outrun the bear, just the guy next to you—I invited my friend Hopper (aka George McDonough), a thirty-five-year-old landscape architect I'd recently met at the Y, to come along. A former Division I swimmer at the University of Rhode Island, he was behind me as far as getting back in shape was concerned—in other words, a little bit slower—and that was a very, very good thing.

"Sure," he answered. "Where?"

He quickly proved a lot more useful than mere shark fodder. Asking him was a godsend—a moment of pure serendipity. He actually thought about stuff like logistics, what would be lightweight, and where we'd have to walk versus swim, and so on. He even thought of what we should tow behind us. We wanted to be self-sufficient and tow everything we needed. I had the bright idea of using a kid's blow-up raft; Hopper had the even brighter idea of a surfboard: low profile, able to hold a lot of weight, and with tail fins to keep it in line.

He came up with a name for our adventure—SwimTrek BVI. And he turned out to be an experienced open-water swimmer, having raced at distances up to eight miles. It was Hopper who suggested we bring duct tape and epoxy for board repair, a VHF radio, a Swiss Army knife, a chart, a couple of pairs of Crocs, and the flag we'd fly above our board to warn away boaters. I came up with resortwear and toothbrushes. In my own defense, I did think of getting us each a pair of Xterra racing wet suits to protect us from *Linuche unguiculata,* the stinging, itching thimble jellyfish that are everywhere you want to be in the Caribbean in the warmer months, but the airline lost that bag on the flight down. (Okay, okay, Hopper actually thought of the idea of the wet suits but I got the company to let us use them for free.)

About the only thing Hopper wasn't prepared for was hostile locals. Our first night in the islands, at a bar near our Tortola hostel, he was laying it on thick with Simon, the bartender, perhaps hoping we'd get a few free drinks, when this good-looking Australian woman overheard us talking about our swim.

"Really?" she joined in, pleasantly enough at first. "That doesn't sound very hard—only a few miles between them."

"I know," Hopper answered. "Although everybody else we've told hasn't believed us."

"It's just twenty miles in a few days," I added. "Anybody could do it."

I was about to get up and stand closer when her entire expression changed. It reminded me of a look my high school water polo cocaptain would get before kicking me in the balls.

"You're liars," she spat out. We both visibly flinched but she wasn't done. "You're not swimming anywhere. Nobody'd be that stupid. Do you know anything about the currents between the islands? You can't swim against them. I've dived in there enough to know. You're a bunch of wankers."

"Oh, no," I replied, raising my eyebrows. "We're definitely doing it."

"Fuckers."

Her curse worked more like a blessing. Our first swim—a two-and-a-half-mile warm-up from the Virgin Gorda ferry landing, in Spanish Town, north to the Little Dix Bay resort—went, well, swimmingly. Our "safety" boat—a twenty-five-foot motorboat captained by photographer Paolo Marchesi and first-mated by his assistant, Derik Olson—didn't turn up. (In fact, they wouldn't appear until later that night, complaining loudly about their SS *Minnow*–quality tub.) Given my nascent shark hysteria, their absence could've been a bad thing. As we began our first leg, I was doing my best Don Knotts imitation—head and neck bobbing all over the place looking for fins—but the scariest thing we passed was some razor-sharp coral just a foot below the surface, with hundreds of *Finding Nemo* fish darting in and out.

Even better, the surfboard was surprisingly easy to handle. Hopper had devised a simple tethering system: a strap buckled around the waist attached to a twelve-foot length of polypropylene rope. Weighing ten pounds and loaded with about forty pounds of our things stuffed in two dry bags, the board definitely slowed the swimmer doing the towing, reducing speed by about a quarter, but even so, we managed to reach Little Dix Bay in just under an hour. As I hinted at in the beginning of this chapter, we emerged from the water Sean Connery style, peeling our goggles off in one fluid movement as we strode through the soft Caribbean sand.

"Nice swim," Hopper said, his uneven smile beaming in the subtropical heat.

A woman lounging in a black bikini looked up and asked, "Where did you two come from?"

"The ferry landing," Hopper answered nonchalantly, unstrapping his dry bag.

"Oh," she said. "But that's a few miles away, isn't it?"

"Yes," Hopper answered. "It is."

"Wow, that's so cool."

That's when the waitress walked by and we ordered Red Stripes and seviche, not martinis. "Name?" she asked, rather sweetly. "Hodding . . . H-O-D-D-I-N-G. Carter," I answered. "Hodding Carter."

Paolo and Derik showed up just in time for dinner that night. Their bags had gotten left behind—in Philly—and they'd waited an extra day in St. Thomas for them. We'd actually met Derik briefly in St. Thomas at the ferry terminal where a drunken, muscled guy had forced some chewed-on chicken bones on Derik and muttered an incantation of sorts. The words had been hard to make out but not the venom with which they were uttered. It proved to be a bit of voodoo, or so their delayed bags and boat troubles suggested. In retrospect, I believe Derik should've tossed the bones back at the crazed fellow. Maybe that would have saved some trouble. But who knows.

Dinner, though, was beyond description. A fitting last meal before heading off on a grand adventure. There were some seven different tables spilling over with seafood; cooked every style imaginable from sushi to seviche to curried, it was there. Between nibbles of conversation, Hopper, the photo boys, and I devoured enough sea life to bring the Black Sea back to life. And it was all free. A publicist for the BVI tourism board had sent out word that we were Olympic swimmers and we were wined and dined in style at every port.

As conversation ensued, we learned that Paolo, originally hailing from Turin, Italy, was a fledgling open-water swimmer who hoped to join us in the water on occasion. He had gargantuanly long feet that soon became the envy of the trip—every great swimmer has long feet. Derik was a down-home Montana lad who'd never been on an ocean and as the night wore on and rum was consumed, along with more shrimp than was proper, his freckles began to look more like thousands of beacons for the harsh tropical sun. *Burn me, burn me,* they beckoned.

Later, after we retired to our sumptuously appointed bungalow, lying in his sumptuous king-size bed, wrapped in a fuzzy white bathrobe, rum drink in hand, Hopper said, unexpectedly, "I feel a lot more confident about our swim. I feel like we're not gonna die."

"That's good," I replied and passed out on the cot next to him.

At six the next morning, however, I wasn't so sure. We were leaving Virgin Gorda for the four-mile swim to Ginger from the Baths, a boulder-strewn volcanic peninsula that looks more like Joshua Tree than the Caribbean. This was where, according to the Australian woman, we'd have our asses handed to us: The ocean has had thousands of miles to build up its tempo before it pounds the rocky windward beach just around the point. Indeed, beyond the peninsula, I was sure a hurricane and more waited for us. I felt like I could see shark fins, roiling whitecaps, and marauding speedboats everywhere. I wanted to go home. End this foolishness before it'd even begun.

"Hey, Hod," Hopper called, casually treading water beside me. "What a perfect day to begin our journey, huh? Let's get going, though. Get this under our belt."

"Yeah, you guys go," Paolo said from the safety of his speedboat, which wasn't turning out to be so speedy. Not only was it impossible to start, it also wouldn't plane. I was sure we'd be half eaten by the time they ever got to us.

Thankfully, Saint Jude, patron saint of lost causes,[3] was smiling down on us: The winds were out of the east-northeast instead of the prevailing southeast, and both the water and the sky were clear and warm. With this particular wind direction, the chain of rocky islands would protect us much of the crossing from the Baths to Ginger, blocking the east wind and creating shallow water most of the way.

We didn't see much. Millions of tiny glistening fish

3. I learned this from watching *The Rookie* so many times. Dennis Quaid wore his image on a chain around his neck in the movie, and as we kicked off, I really wished I had my own.

streaked along the surface, so small they seemed more optical illusions than aquatic life, and a couple of barracuda swam urgently toward us and then appeared to back up when they saw our size, as if thinking, *Oops—my bad.* That was it, if you discount the hundreds of jellyfish attacking us. For an animal that has no brain, bones, eyes, or heart, the thimble jelly is a tricky little predator, filled with stinging cells called nemocysts that inject their venom into you with teeny-tiny harpoons. I really didn't like them.

As the minutes, a half hour, and then an hour ticked off and the water got deeper and deeper, I grew ever more freaked out, despite our mother hens, Paolo and Derik, constantly hovering within a few hundred yards. For some reason, I was most afraid of sharks in the deeper water, although most attacks happen in shallow areas and, even more pertinent, my own not-so-casual research showed that there have been only four unprovoked shark attacks in the Virgin Islands in the past one hundred years. Even so, I took comfort in the fact that Hopper was in the rear, pulling the surfboard. Sharks would attack from behind, right?

Suddenly, Hopper stopped swimming. We were about a quarter mile off Ginger Island in one hundred feet of water. Not a good place for a chat.

"We gotta do something different," he said, taking a swig from the water bottle that had been strapped to the board.

"Why would we do that? Let's keep going," I answered, a little pissy. "We're nearly there."

"We're not going anywhere. I've been watching that white scar on the cliffs over there for ten minutes. We haven't moved."

Now that we were no longer in the lee of the outlying islands, those whitecaps I'd imagined had become very real, along with an accompanying fifteen-knot wind. Although theoretically, the wind shouldn't have been working against us, because of land shapes and the funneling caused by the channels, the wind was blowing almost straight at us. Also, the one-knot current our chart indicated was more like two to three. Our destination on Ginger—a lagoon behind a northeast peninsula—was now upwind.

We hastily slipped on our Zura Alphas, flexible, lightweight fins that would give us just enough of an advantage to compensate for the wind and current. Except they didn't.

We swam for another ten minutes, but we were still going backward.

Clearly outpowered, we decided to put the wind on our port beam—our left hip—and head for the less desirable north shore, where a boat appeared to be anchored. Maybe they'd have some food. In our haste, we'd forgotten to pack more than an apple and water that morning.

Fifteen minutes later, we literally tumbled ashore, arriving like bewildered shipwreck survivors as breakers sent us rolling over spiny sea urchins. What had looked like an inviting beach from four hundred yards away turned out to be a fifteen-foot-deep beach of broken coral—sharp, merciless detritus probably killed by humans in some way or another. And the boat that was going to be our salvation was actually a wrecked charter sailboat, itself forlornly waiting to be rescued.

That's how we spent our afternoon — forlornly waiting as well. While Paolo and Derik went back to Virgin Gorda to get their boat fixed, Hopper and I swam another mile to the western edge of the island and generally wilted in the inescapable sun. That evening, minutes before dusk, they finally returned with food, drinks, and a still-broken boat.

"Well, day two down and no shark. That's a good thing," I said, toasting our success with a bit of rum-spiked Gatorade.

Derik looked at Paolo, as if to ask, *Should we tell him?* and then said, "Paolo did see this really big thing come up behind you once."

"How big?" I asked.

"Really big," Paolo said, smiling. "And it was definitely a shark."

That night, camping through two storms on the beach without a sleeping bag, rain jacket, or even a tarp, I dreamed of shark-shaped jellyfish eating holes through my sodden brain. I vainly tried to squeeze under the surfboard for protection and the only thing that made me happy was watching Hopper trying to hide from the rain, huddled under a fish crate.

Day three was a short two-mile but deep water swim from Ginger to the Cooper Island Beach Club. Practicing good stroke mechanics and head positioning, I would stare straight down, and what I saw wasn't pretty—it was *gorgeous*—an endless expanse of dreamy blue water. I knew I was looking at least as far as 40, maybe 50, feet deep, but the milky blueness was so uniform in this 120-foot water, I couldn't see anything. No bottom, no fish, no nothing, except for an occasional terrifying strand of seaweed darting into view that never failed to make me jump.

Slowly, though, we were developing a certain rhythm—and not just in the water.

"I've figured out the ebb and flow of this trip," Hopper said the next morning while I fried up a batch of holes-in-the-wall (fried egg inside a hollowed out slice of bread) in our little kitchenette at the down-to-earth resort. He was looking and sounding a little stressed. I was feeling the same. "The tension builds as the swim approaches," he went on. "You're wondering about the variables, the current, the wind, boats, and so on, and then you're a little bit freaked out when you first shove off. Things start to mellow as your arms loosen up. You're under way. Life is good. Then you arrive and you're all elated. You have a beer, sleep, go over the swim, and then it's just . . . a slow . . . build . . . toward . . . that . . . preswim tension."

The best part of swimtrekking, as we were now calling it, was that, unlike 99 percent of the swimmers in the world, we actually arrived somewhere at the end of our workouts and talked to real people. As Gary Hall Jr. once said, "It's bad enough talking to the stripe at the bottom of the pool. It's even worse when it starts talking back." The other good thing about swimtrekking was that it was making me a lot stronger. Perhaps everybody training for the Olympics should take up loaded-surfboard pulling.

On Salt Island, a brief stopover between Cooper and Peter Islands on the grueling fourth day of our voyage, we came ashore to find a skeletal elderly man wandering outside the ramshackle cinder-block huts that clutter the shoreline, looking somewhat befuddled in his slightly askew construction helmet. His name was Henry Leonard, he said, and he lived there all by himself. There used to be families scattered all over the one-and-a-half-square-mile island, he explained, collecting salt in the inland ponds. Now it was just him, the rustling palms, and the salt, which stretched behind his shack in a long, uninterrupted sheet of gray. We talked for a few more minutes, but then we, too, had to shove off. Henry's scene was a little too lonely, maybe a little too close to home, reminding me just how isolated I could end up if I kept running off on this quest of mine.

The six-mile Cooper to Peter leg was our longest by far, almost the equivalent in effort of running a marathon. And it was already ten a.m., and we still had four miles to go. Hopper and I swam off without Paolo and Derik, but after half an hour and no safety boat, Hopper tapped me on the shoulder. "What do you want to do?" he asked. "Turn back? Wait here?" Surely they'd show up any minute.

Mere seconds later, I was staring again into that never-ending nothingness, screaming to myself, *Turn back! This is how it's gonna end!* But I kept swimming. After about an hour and no bites to our soft underbellies, I noticed that I was no longer jumping like a frightened surface minnow at every perceived attack. I even started hoping that Paolo and Derik wouldn't show up. I was feeling like part of the ocean, as if I actually belonged in it instead of being a temporary, wary visitor. The wind, now stronger, pushed us down the ever-towering swells. I was Aquaman, Johnny Weissmuller, and a dolphin rolled into one!

I was so happy, I didn't even mind the harbor attendant yelling that we couldn't swim near the boats at the Peter Island Resort dock. When we explained to him that we were a boat, he just waved exasperatedly toward a ladder hanging unadorned beside a sybaritic fifty-foot cruiser.

High on endorphins, we zipped around Peter Island's luxurious digs, playing on Hobie Cats, downing some rum again, and getting massaged on a hilltop overlooking nearly all the Virgin Islands. And we were just one day away from the Willy T.

Our last morning, we had a tailwind, making our final goal—a floating bar called the Willy T—absurdly do-able. The *William Thornton*, a hundred-foot steel schooner moored in a bay called the Bight on Norman Island, is party central for the Virgin Islands, a place where women jump naked from the railing to get a free T-shirt and men get drunk trying to urge the women to do so. "No matter what you do," one friend had demanded, "you gotta finish at the Willy T."

It was a five-mile swim that felt like less than one. Time in the water no longer represented worrying about survival. It was simply what we did—where we belonged. We were the SwimTrek BVI boys, and the ocean was our playground.

When we rounded Water Point, a jutting peninsula on Norman's northwestern edge and the entrance to the Bight, we passed over some divers forty to fifty feet below us—a surreal experience, to suddenly run into other humans flippering through our sea. Their bubbles bumped into us, drifting to the surface. And then we saw the Willy T itself, about a third of a mile away on the far side of the bay. Without exchanging a word, we decided to race that last stretch to touch the hull, which we did, simultaneously.

"We just swam from Virgin Gorda!" Hopper announced. He was answered with cheers and a couple of free beers.

Zeus, the horniest bartender outside of Tom Cruise in *Cocktail*, poured us a couple of painkillers—double shots of rum hidden in a masterly mix of coconut, pineapple, and orange juices—when we made it up to the bow. Actually, that first beer had gotten to me, so I don't know if the bar was in the bow or the stern, but I do know it was near an end.

As the afternoon passed, more and more revelers arrived by boat—beers in hand, bodies bobbing to the bar music, heavy on rap, reggae, and sexy R&B. Even the women seemed like predators, waiting to see who would get the most debauched. Silent old men (older than me) stood along the railing, praying somebody would go for a

T-shirt. As we got drunker, Zeus seemed more and more impressed with our swim, but when I asked if we could get free T-shirts, he said, "No way, man. That's for the women, and there's only one way they're getting them: they've got to show Zeus the stuff." Then he turned up the season's hit song, "Temperature," so loud that even the sea seemed to vibrate.

As if on cue, an attractive newlywed from South Carolina zipped up in a boat with her husband and, after downing a few of her own painkillers, got herself a tattoo. This required the bride to lift her shirt, so that Zeus could lick the skin just above her left nipple. You know, so he could wet a spot for applying the temporary tattoo. Her husband, powering down a Red Stripe, yelled out, "That's what I'm talking about!"

I chugged down another painkiller, gave Hopper a kiss, and smiled, a contented man. I was finally a professional swimmer.

Seven

A Long Ways Off

After returning from SwimTrek BVI, I felt like a god, at least in the water, almost like I had back in my college senior year. I was doing sets I hadn't been able to manage the past few years and I knew that if I could taper one more time, I'd be a hell of a lot closer to those Trials' cutoffs. Instead of tapering, though, I got sick—first with some kind of stomach bug and then the flu. I ended up staying out of the water for nearly three weeks.

One thing that all masters swimmers had in common was the litany of excuses. Much like an undergraduate degree is to a PhD, excuses were a necessary precursor to racing at a masters meet. If you didn't have at least a good half dozen ready and waiting, you weren't a real masters swimmer. Cowboys and rednecks might lean against the fence railing, staring across the horizon, occasionally spitting chew. Masters swimmers stood before each other, pulling their foot up to their butt or touching their toes with straightened legs, and listed in detail all the things wrong with them, making it seem a near miracle they were even able to dive in the pool.

"Hey, Andy, how's it going?" I'd ask.

"Okay, and you."

"Well, I tore my left ACL last week and had ortho surgery over the weekend but I think that 104 fever I had last night has at least dropped down to 101 or so. I don't think I'll be able to do my best," I would answer.

"Geez, Hodding, that's too bad. Almost as bad as my appendectomy," Andy would answer. "The doctor said I shouldn't swim for at least a month but I thought I'd give it a whirl anyway. And did I tell you? My contractor put a lien on my house, painted our house the wrong color, and slept with Janey. Hey, could you zip up my suit?"

Truly, though, when I was finally well, I couldn't get back into a daily routine because life caught up to me. Even Lisa didn't need to remind me: I needed to make money. To this end, I started writing about anything I could think of: my daughter's pet pig, smoking Boston mackerel in a homemade smoker, the history of orthopedics, my biggest marital mistakes, etc. — pretty much anything that anybody wanted me to. Pursuing Olympic gold was the furthest thing from my mind but I still managed a few workouts, here and there.

Then sometime in May, George Pond, an old friend from Kenyon College, called and told me to take a look at the national masters rankings for the 50 free. He'd beaten me by three-hundredths of a second and was ranked one place ahead of me. While gloating to no end, he also claimed that he went even faster while leading off a relay at an alumni meet held in Kenyon's brand-new state-of-the-art pool.

Before he even got off the line, I was on the Maine Masters Web site, furiously searching for the next meet. As luck would have it, there was one last short-course-yards meet, the Black Fly Invitational, about eight days away, and I set my sights on it, planning to wipe his name off the national rankings. I tapered off of nothing, meaning I sprinted for a few days and then rested. Even more desperately, I decided to shave down — removing all body hair has been shown to decrease drag and reduce a swimmer's overall stroke count by as much as one stroke per length of a pool. And I still would wear my tech suit.

I was going to beat George, my junior by three years, no matter what.

The only problem was that I was attempting to do so in one of Maine's slowest competitive pools. The water is extremely shallow — three feet at one end — creating unusually large waves to plow through. Also, after my sicknesses, I was no longer in the shape I needed to be.

Out of desperation, I changed my sprint stroke, dropping the hip swiveling and going for all-out turnover. My arms were like propellers, they were revolving so fast. I had myself timed for a 25 free — one length of the pool — and clocked a scorching 9.9 seconds. If I could keep up that tempo, I'd break 21 in the 50, putting me within tenths of going fast enough for the Olympic Trials.[1]

---

1. Again, you can't qualify for the trials by swimming in races that are in twenty-five-yard pools, since the Olympics are contested in fifty-meter pools, but you can convert your times with a fair amount of accuracy.

The day of the meet, I shaved down, drove to Ellsworth, slipped on my Fastskin—and sucked, big time. Problem was, in retrospect, I was doing a good imitation of a sprinter, but I was not a sprinter. Even if I had been doing things properly, I couldn't maintain an effective stroke at the tempo I was following for each stroke of my arms. I demonstrably slowed down in the last five yards, so much so that even Mike Schmidt, whose specialty is the mile, almost caught up to me. I swam a 22.7—much worse than I had at the New England Masters.

Once again, I found myself asking, *What am I doing?* Why was I wasting so much time in the pool to swim like that? I kept swimming after that meet but barely. I'd show up a few times a week and swim some lackluster laps. And that was it.

Not only did I sink into a mild depression but also I intentionally let all the lessons learned at the Race Club slip away. I decided I knew best and that my straight-arm underwater pull was what I needed to concentrate on—not some gimmicky, hippie hip-swiveling fad. Of course, it wasn't the hip-snap that produced such dispiriting results but somehow I lumped it into that failed experience. So, not only did I not swim as much as I needed in the following months, but when I did, I failed to do it properly.

I had committed to swimming relays with some other Maine swimmers at the World Masters Championships, however, and I showed up for them at Stanford University in Palo Alto, California, in early August 2006. For most older swimmers, this was the main event—the yearly get-together where the world's fastest old people felt like kids once again. More than three thousand men and women turned out for Worlds and I'd never seen so many elderly hard bodies in my entire life. By elderly I mean anything from twenty-five to one hundred. There were some eye-poppingly beautiful women and men. I had to shake myself out of staring again and again. Soon, while wandering around the two outdoor Olympic-length pools, I found myself muttering over and over, while seeing yet another fifty-five-year-old man with abs of steel, "Oh, yeah, he's not on steroids!" It was a vain attempt not to feel inferior. And who knows, maybe they were doping. It was a giant meat market and everything looked like prime rib. Although Joel Stager had convinced me that people are able to gain muscle in their latter years, I was sure that many of these people were cheating. Since 99.9 percent of masters swimmers are not a threat to the younger world-record-setting swimmers, no one checks us for using illegal performance-enhancing substances. Considering these bodies and some of the shockingly fast times, I was convinced the elder set had discovered HGH.

Obviously, I didn't have a very good experience at Worlds. I told myself it wasn't my meet. It wasn't why I was swimming. I needed to wait for the real competitions. Pretty lame excuses for a masters swimmer; the truth was, there were lots of older swimmers doing some amazing swimming. There were dozens of men who could beat me, or at the very least push me. Why hadn't I come prepared?

I don't know but it did feel like old home week. My new Maine friends were there, including Mike Schmidt. He was becoming my masters version of Frankie Franklin, the kid who kept swimming faster than me when I was a boy in Mississippi. I turned to Mike via e-mail for workouts and advice, but I also couldn't help feeling he was my nemesis. We were nearly exactly the same age and had swum against each other in college. He'd gone to Oakland University, a Division II powerhouse in Michigan, and we'd actually competed against each other in a couple of duel meets back in the eighties. We were two big fish in Maine's small pond. We had staked out our ends of the competitive territory, but when we crossed over and swam a race that mattered to both of us — the 200 free, for instance — the tension was palpable, which was actually a surprising (but fun) thing to have at age forty-four.

His very existence got me up at 4:30 a.m. just to work out and helped me feel younger. Having a racing nemesis was the closest thing to feeling like I was still that college-age kid that deep down I knew I still was. Our confrontations were never so obvious as butting heads or ribbing each other — exactly the opposite, actually. We usually wouldn't say anything when these events came up — unlike all the trash we'd throw at each other otherwise. We'd keep quiet, respectful. So it made me happy to see his bald, grinning head peering through the crowded grandstand at Stanford's Avery Aquatic Center. Also there were Doug Pride, a high school math teacher who was an incredible sprinter and nice guy; Lee Lindenau, a pharmacist with a deceptively fast breaststroke; Andy Pulsifer, a momentarily retired college swim coach with one of the smoothest strokes I've seen and a record-setting middle-distance and distance swimmer; Kevin Crowley, a surprise in that he wasn't a national-level competitor; and Bill Rupert, my sixty-three-year-old roommate, who spoke in elliptical sentences and usually forgot where his room was. Bill unsuccessfully tried to teach me not to worry about my times but succeeded at teaching me how to rewire my stove outlet during a power outtage so the generator could run everything. It's illegal but effective.

Plenty of others showed up, too, including John Fields, my camp buddy, and Gary Hall Sr., also my camp buddy. John and Gary both had a great meet—damn them. John took third place a couple of times in his age group and Gary set a pair of world records in the backstroke in the 55–59 age group.

In fact, almost everybody I knew ended up swimming well. All their old buddies from college were there and nobody wanted to be shown up. The only good thing that happened to me, however, was that I finally got to eat at an In-N-Out Burger. I'd recently read an article about the California chain in the *New York Times* and my mouth had been watering the entire flight out in anticipation. The place is so un–fast food–like that even Eric Schlosser, author of *Fast Food Nation*, likes it. Nothing cost more than $2.50. They offer only four items to eat—hamburger, cheeseburger, Double-Double burger, and hand-cut fries—and everything is made from scratch. And I wasn't disappointed. I wolfed down two Double-Double burgers my first evening out there, sighing out loud over the grilled onions and fresh-cut french fries. I wanted to move. Later, I brought my roommate, Bill, and he declared it the best burger he'd ever had.

My other favorite moment came on my last night when Andy Pulsifer, Bill, a lanky Italian named Lorenzo, a friend of Andy's named Chip, and I wandered the streets of Santa Cruz looking for fish tacos. Chip kept complaining about the delay as we trudged in and out of yet another Mexican joint that didn't have any such tacos, because he had an important race the next day, but Andy was a man on a mission. He'd eaten one a few nights before, declared it heavenly, and now had to share the experience. We eventually found a place serving them and they were very good: crispy and juicy, well worth the four miles we'd walked.

Oh, yeah. I was there for a swim meet, too. In the pool my best moments came in the relays. In fact, our 200 free relay of Mike, Doug, Andy, and me took sixth place out of seventy-one or so relay entrants in the 160–199 age group (they combine ages for relays to create age groups). Sixth place in the world, even against a bunch of old fogies, was pretty darn good. Practically the only teams that beat us were ones carefully pieced together with the best swimmers from around the world. We went up against an Italian national relay and one called Team TYR, an American effort comprised of the fastest guys in the country in their forties—a group that I was currently *not* a part of. It felt heartwarming that four guys from Maine, one of the least populated states in the country, could do so well.

TYR is a competitive swimming outfitter and its sponsorship got me to thinking. What if our relay started training together and went for the world record. Could we get Viagra as a sponsor? Why hadn't anybody else thought of that? We could put their logo right across our crotch. On second thought, maybe it wasn't such an ingenious idea.

My individual races stunk. My worst showing was thirty-fourth, in the 100 free, and my best was somewhere in the teens. Considering how many old people beat me just in my category, it was clear I was a long ways off even qualifying for the Trials. Lisa's questions, while not meant to hurt, just drove the knife deeper. One night, when I called to report my results, she asked, "So are all these guys who beat you also training for the Olympics?" And a bit later, after I'd answered "no" to that one, she asked, "If you can't beat the people your own age, why do you think you can beat anyone younger?"

"Jesus, Lisa. Why'd you ask that? Are you mad I'm not home helping?"

"Look, if you don't want me to take an interest in what you're doing, just say so. I thought maybe it was some sort of plan," she added.

☙ ☙ ☙

The day I returned home, I swam three miles in a local lake (the Y was closed), and ever since, I've made every day count. Sometimes I have to be beaten over the head with a lesson and, regrettably, this was one of those times. I'm not too sure what had been going on before Worlds—why I had slacked off so tremendously—but clearly I couldn't let that happen again, mainly because I couldn't handle Lisa asking such painful, soul-searching questions. I had less than two years to qualify for the Trials at that point and I finally realized that I had to make every day, nearly every workout, count.

I still believed I could make it to the Trials and maybe, with a little bit of luck, the Olympics. I hadn't given it my all and, I decided while flying back East, I hadn't been concentrating enough on racing the right event. Back in college, my coach had made me swim the 50 and 100 free races because we didn't have enough sprinters. Before that year, I'd been a skinny, kick-the-sand-in-my-face, slow-twitch-muscle kind of guy. Asking me to sprint had been like asking George Foreman to box as a featherweight. It was nearly a physical impossibility. Yet, within the year, I was one of our top sprinters. Sitting on that plane, I decided it was time for one more session with Coach Steen, the reigning king of NCAA Division III swimming. He'd turned me, a dreamer, into a national champion back in 1984. Maybe he could do it one more time.

It was time to repeat my senior year.

Eight

Going to Nationals

Why senior year? I always thought it saved my life — or at least my sanity.

I had been in a two-year, one-sided relationship with a girl who had graduated the previous year. To say I liked her would be like saying John Hinckley had a crush on Jodie Foster. I worshipped her. I'm not sure how she felt about me. She said she loved me and I'm sure it was true on some level. Mainly, though, I think she let me hang around so long because I made life in Gambier, Ohio, tolerable for her. She hated it there: its size, its insularity, and most of all, its distance from New York City.

Perhaps, though, she loved me the way any twenty-year-old loves another young adult and it was I that had things out of whack. I didn't think about relationships or women the same way most guys did. I didn't go around saying things like, "I wouldn't kick her out of bed." Instead, I thought, "I'd like to settle into a thirty-year mortgage with her." Ever since my parents split up when I was fourteen, my one life goal had been to find my true love, marry, and then happily stay with my beloved until death did us part. I wanted to show my divorced parents the proper way to do things. Picture a male Cinderella with a mean streak of vengeance. I was the male embodiment of a fairy-tale-addled sixteen-year-old girl. As a result, I placed unbearable pressure on this relationship and followed my girlfriend around like a lost Labrador puppy. In turn, she would break up with me every six months, and I'd spend days and/or weeks begging her to get back together with me. Our relationship was about as steady as Don Knott's Adam's apple in *The Ghost and Mr. Chicken.*

Only one thing gave me any confidence. I *knew* she liked me because I was a swimmer. How could it be otherwise? We swimmers were the campus studs (at least that's what *we* thought) because we'd won national championships four years in a row. The fact that I was merely an alternate on that national team didn't matter and the fact that she often asked me things like, "Why are you guys always hugging and touching each other? It's weird," was insignificant. I knew deep down she dug my Speedo.

Yet, when she graduated from Kenyon a year ahead of me and started living in Boston, thus requiring me to make frequent trips from the Midwest to the East Coast, I considered quitting swimming. How else could I keep her? Swimming had defined me since I was five years old, but I'd sacrifice it all to keep her by my side. After an assortment of panic attacks, freak outs, and frantic flights to Boston, I told Coach Steen that I was thinking about quitting swimming so I could go see my girlfriend more often.

"Hoddo, it's your decision. She is a fine young woman," he said in his raspy, high-pitched tone—acquired from decades of yelling at water-deafened swimmers. "You've got to do what you think is best for you. I'm not going to lie to you—I think it's a mistake. But if you decide not to spend all your free time chasing her through Boston and try to stick with the team, I'm not going to let you back on unless it's a full commitment. It has to be all the way or nothing. Otherwise you're just wasting everybody's time."

Well, the choice was obvious. I was going with my heart. I went out to see her the following weekend, scheduling my absence from school during the team's first meeting of the preseason to make sure Coach knew what I'd decided. The visit was similar to most of our get-togethers those days: We went for runs around Fresh Pond. Ate some good food. Did what most young adults do—all while I worried about our relationship, and for good reason. Before falling asleep, once again she wondered if we should break up.

I distinctly remember enjoying a cooling breeze that sneaked through the bedroom window when the sixth full-on panic attack in the last six weeks hit me. I'd been having them ever since the last time she'd broken up with me. I thought that I was losing my mind as I imagined the walls closing in on me and that if I told anybody about it, they'd lock me away in the nuthouse (therapy was not big in my family back then). By this point, the attacks had become closer to me than some of my own family members and I knew what was going on. My hands grew clammy, my face turned white, and I waited for that wave of sheer terror to roll through me. Moments later, it did.

Having now dealt with these attacks for so many weeks, though, I knew what to do. Instead of literally clinging to the corner of a wall as I'd done the first time, I quickly tried to think of all the things I might be repressing: was there a God, was Grenada no longer a safe place to go to med school, was Cap'n Crunch better than Frosted Flakes? I rapidly examined each concern, reassured myself that not knowing the answers to some was okay, and yet I still didn't feel better. Any moment I was going to die.

What else could be bothering me?

Oh, yeah: Was she going to break up with me again?

Well, was she, I wondered? How would it feel? Shitty. What could I do about it? Nothing. . . . And then it came to me: I could break up with her and end this insane roller coaster ride. Free her and, more importantly at that moment, free myself from all this fear. I really was going to end up in an institution if I didn't.

And so I did.

The morning after returning to Ohio, I shuffled into Coach's office and asked if it was too late for me to return to the team.

"It has to be all the way or nothing. That's our deal,

right?" he asked, eyeing me almost like an opponent—a little open wariness that he'd never shown before. In the past, ever since I stopped midrace during our intra-squad meet my freshman year, Coach had never bothered to be wary of me because he didn't bother with me at all. I was not up to snuff and it didn't matter to him that I had a fever of 103 and an undiagnosed case of mono during that race. I'd failed.

"And you have to lift weights and attend every morning practice. You skip either one, you don't swim. It's that simple."

And that's what I did. For the first time in years I put swimming in the forefront and I lifted weights. I didn't skip practices. Mike Solomon and Brian Horgan, two seniors on the team who'd been just two of my many friends in the past, were now my best friends. We slumped around the campus at five a.m. together. We went from barely squatting 150 pounds to doing many reps of 350 pounds.

"Come on, you can do it. Urgh!" we'd scream at each other and then slap our skinny arms together in an extended high-five.

I think I even set up Brian with his future wife and I spent hours wondering how useful Mike's skill of touching the top of his nose with his tongue might be. I took on a sort of protégé, my friend George Pond—the one who'd recently called me after beating me in the 50. In truth, I was probably more his and Craig Hummer's (another freshman) underling, because they taught me how to have fun in practice again. With them, practice went from a dreaded daily torture session, akin to willfully submitting to repeated nose-hair plucking, to playtime. We'd swim fast—much faster than I or practically any other Kenyon swimmer had ever swum in practice before—but we'd also go running, screaming across the pool deck, kickboards in hand, fly through the air ten feet out, and land with a giant splash, yelling out our favorite superhero. For some reason, those days I was fixated on the Daredevil. I think because he was always having girlfriend problems.

I stopped drinking after the New Year like Coach requested, a big deal for me back then. And I repeated to myself on a daily basis, *Do it all the way or don't bother doing it at all.* I was so clueless, I thought I'd invented the concept, and for a short period I fell in love with *The Fountainhead.*[1]

Despite all my earlier years of dreaming about Olympic glory, I'd never fully invested myself beyond a few weeks here and there. I hadn't known what it took and I didn't have the kind of parents that pushed me or taught me how to succeed at all cost. I loved the feeling of no longer having any excuses, knowing that I was giving something my all. Without my being fully aware, it was a little bit scary even, and so I naturally grew closer with those people going through the same experience. These days, there's only

---

1. Ayn Rand has a powerful, unnatural sway over many a young adult who's trying to cut his/her path.

one thing that I habitually miss in my life, and it's those days, those fellow swimmers, and that particular feeling of unrestrained effort.

As the year progressed, I got a little faster and I had visible muscles for the first time in my life. The only real indicator that something unusual was happening, though, was that I puked after racing the 200 free sometime in January. The time I posted that day wasn't astounding but it was within three seconds of my best time. Considering that I usually swam about six seconds slower than my best time in season, I knew I was going to be faster at the end of the year. But there were no record-setting times: no one was asking to put me on a box of Wheaties, and for good reason. I was on a team that worked hard through the season, never resting or cutting back on yardage for a dual meet. The theory was that when you tapered for the big meet at the end of the season, you'd go even faster — over-compensation, it was called. I prayed for that day, but in the meantime, I was doing much better than previous years, unrested.

We tapered for the conference meet, the one where I was going to try and get my qualifying times for Nationals. Then, I got horribly sick two days before the meet. I had a fever and skipped practice. I was lying on my back, feeling sorry for myself, when Mike and Brian came banging on my apartment door. Mike seemed especially worried.

"Come on, Hodding," he pleaded. "It's all in your head. You're okay. Just come swim. You need to keep your feel of the water, loser."

For his sake, I walked the two miles to the other end of campus where our two-year-old but dreary pool was. I climbed in and . . . like I'd told him. I couldn't swim. After the first 200 yards of warm-up, I was pooped. I crawled out.

It was over. All that work, wasted. The first day of conferences was in two days and there was no way I'd fully recover. I wasn't any better the following day.

The day after, I arrived at conferences (it had some longer name that indicated our region, but this is what we called it) in Oberlin, Ohio, with considerably lowered expectations, hoping that I could at least salvage all those hard months of work by making it to Nationals in my best race: the 200 freestyle. The moment I dove in, though, I could tell something had changed for the better. I didn't feel great but I was better.

When I swam day-to-day, I felt like anybody else. The water was heavy and I had to push my way through just as much as glide. In short, there was a constant, palpable struggle. I would have to remind myself to stretch it out, slip through the water, overcome the instinct to thrash. That day, as each lap went by, I slid through the water unconsciously. It gurgled and slipped by me as if I was covered in oil. I could still feel the weakening effects of whatever bug I'd caught but my taper was doing its best to defeat the virus.

Evidently, the taper won. Not only did I win a couple of races, but I qualified for Nationals in all three of my events: the 50, 100, and 200 freestyles. For three years,

I'd watched with ever-increasing envy as other swimmers won their chance to compete at Nationals, fulfilling practically every Kenyon swimmer's destiny. The previous year, I'd even qualified in the 200, but Coach hadn't needed me. Our team had that much depth of talent. This time, though, there was no denying me. It was mine. I was finally going.

While the rest of campus fled for spring break, my fellow swimmers and I had the run of campus for the next two and a half weeks in preparation for Nationals. Close from training together all year, including nearly two weeks together in Florida, we now grew even closer. And giddy. We felt unbound thanks not only to the melting snow, but also to our extended taper. Every day, Coach cautioned us not to attempt flying off a roof or, more likely, sneaking in a game of pick-up basketball. I'd thought I'd been rested for conferences, but with each passing day, I felt more and more akin to the superheroes my freshmen friends and I had pretended to be during the regular season. Up, up, and away.

We flew down to Nationals in Atlanta in mid-March determined to win the Lords' fifth national title, even though my senior class was probably the weakest that Coach had fielded in quite a while.

I'd always looked askance at many of the traditions of our team, priding myself on my nonconformity. I had always clapped weakly when we did the cadenced clap for each letter of KENYON LORDS. I didn't wear my team T-shirt with that year's slogan. At conferences, when we counted out the number of years we'd won it—some twenty-eight, I believe, by my senior year—I usually just mouthed the words. So I was surprised when I found myself asking Chris Cunningham and Peter Loomis to help me shave my head. The Lords had been shaving theirs for years, and for years I had said that if there was one thing I never was going to do, it was shave my head. But there I was, staring into the motel mirror as Chris and Peter hovered over me with buzzing clippers and then slickened razors, making me the most hairless Carter male ever.

Did I look good.

Mike, Brian, George, and maybe Craig Hummer and I also started a new tradition—getting an earring. These days, that's about as humdrum as you can get, but back then, and especially in the middle of Ohio, it was big stuff, putting us in the realm of uncontrollable youth, or at least sort of "dangerous" guys. However anybody else saw it, we were setting ourselves apart, giving physical representation perhaps to what we'd done all year—set ourselves apart from others on campus and all the other swimmers at Nationals.

And, boy, did it work—that, and all the training we'd gone through. The next morning, diving into the pool for warm-ups, with my scalped dome and hairless body, I was a finely forged Samurai sword, slicing through the waves. The water didn't stand a chance.

Because I qualified for the 200 freestyle as our third fastest swimmer, Coach Steen put me on the 800 freestyle relay in the preliminaries on the first day of the meet. Except, he put me third. In relays, generally, the fastest guy is positioned last, the second fastest first, the third fastest second. The slowest guy goes third. I was a little hurt but was also just happy I'd made the relay, even if it was only the preliminaries.

When I dove in, our relay was in third place. As long as I held ground, we'd be fine. We just wanted to qualify in the top four so we could get a good lane for finals (the faster swimmers get the middle lanes, the slower ones take the outside). I dove in, holding back a bit on the first one hundred, and then turning it all on for the final four laps. Something was wrong, though, and the last fifty felt too easy. Maybe I'd held back too much. I began to worry that I'd ruined my chances of making the finals relay. As I touched the wall with a bit too much steam left in my engine, not wanting to see Coach's patented you're-no-longer-there stare, I hopped out of the pool and looked up at my teammates, who were studying the electronic timing board hanging on the far wall. Seconds passed and then they simply stared back. I was expecting it from the coach but not them. Then, George, my toothpick-skinny freshman friend, slapped me on the back.

"Way to go, Hoddo," he said, and then told me my split. I'd swum my best time by three seconds. I was the fastest guy on our team.

That night, I swam the final leg of the relay, dropping my time by another second, and we won handily. Coach came hurrying over, staring at the scoreboard to double-check things. As I climbed out of the pool, he wrapped me in his bearlike arms and kissed me on the lips.

"You did it," he said, loud enough for the entire pool to hear. "Hoddo, you did it." I went on to take second overall in the individual 200 free (clocking the second-fastest time by a Kenyon swimmer up to that point), as well as first on the 400 free relay. It was my crowning athletic achievement, and near the end of the meet, I found myself crying in the locker room, overwhelmed by all I'd gone through that year. While I wasn't the most emotionally mature twenty-one-year-old, even I was aware what swimming had done for me that year. It and Coach not only taught me how to set and achieve a goal, they also saved my sanity. I was back on my feet, ready to tackle the rest of life.

❧ ❧ ❧

Now, with the Olympic Trials just a year and a half away, I clearly needed to recapture some of that old Kenyon / Jim Steen magic, so in the fall of 2006, I decided to return to Ohio for the first time since 1987.[2] I worked out a deal with the alumni office: I could practice with the team for a week, as long as I agreed to sleep in a dorm, take classes, pretend I was student, and write an article for the alumni magazine.

The only hitch was getting Coach's permission, which took a little effort. Ever the puppet master, he initially

---

2. I graduated in 1984 but came back for a month in the winter of 1987 so that Jim could help me figure out how and where I should train during my post–Peace Corps Olympic bid.

didn't want me to mess with the team's dynamic, worried that letting an "outsider" train with the Lords might devalue what they do. Also, his only brother was very sick with cancer in Massachusetts and Coach really didn't need one more distraction. But eventually, he relented. I was off to college.

♋ ♋ ♋

I was a little nervous about going back, but how hard could this be? What harm could befall me within the safe environs of a college campus? I was an adventurer, after all. I'd sailed a Viking ship in the Arctic, slept in a canoe surrounded by alligators in the Everglades, and crawled through London's sewers to write a book about plumbing. Kenyon would be a piece of cake.

I still felt this was true, even when I discovered upon arriving at Port Columbus International Airport that I'd rented a muscle-bound, fiery-red 2006 Mustang. Sure, it practically shrieked, "Midlife Crisis Loser!" but I could pull it off. I was going to the Olympic Trials, after all. Besides, Kenyon's a walking campus. I could park it somewhere discreet and nobody would be the wiser.

As I drove past dried-up cornfields and the same old turn-offs where local sheriffs had gleefully ticketed me for speeding, a general malaise began to creep over my body. The closer I got to the campus, the more I began to feel like that same nervous wreck of a freshman that I'd been in the fall of 1980. By the time I turned up the hill that gave one a feeling of Kenyon towering over its environs, I wanted to turn back.

"Sweet ride," the mutton-chopped kid said as I struggled out of the car. Instead of parking the MCL (Midlife Crisis Loser) Mobile in some back alley, I'd been forced to plant myself right along Middle Path for all the campus to see. His smirk was as wide as the gulf of a generation.

I was back at Kenyon, for the first time in more than twenty years. And it immediately felt both awful and delightful—in other words, as if I'd never left.

❧ ❧ ❧

Kenyon was founded in 1824 by roving bishop and educator Philander Chase to teach Episcopal clergy who would minister to the West. It was meant to be an unassuming alternative to New York's General Theological Seminary and all its East Coast trappings. He argued, "Unless we can have some little means of educating our pious men here, and here being secure of their affections, station them in our woods and among our scattered people, to gather in and nourish our wandering lambs, we have no reason to hope in the continuance of the Church in the west." He wanted to create a self-sustaining institution in which students would not be swayed by urban enticements.

When I went to Kenyon back in the early eighties, the college had given up on fortifying wayward metaphorical ungulates as well as farming its own food, but it was definitely free of most urban vices, or urban anything for that matter. The surrounding town's population was in the hundreds and there probably wasn't a caffe latte within a hundred miles.

And on this cold, gray December afternoon, had things changed? Glancing around, I had to laugh at the question itself. Central Gambier, with the alumni office, Kenyon Inn, the Deli, post office, and Village Market—looked exactly the same, except for the new coffee shop where I thought the KC used to be. It was almost as if I'd stepped back in time. Hell, I *had* stepped back in time. After getting my classroom assignments, room key, and bedding at the alumni office, I was about to be late for swim practice.

First, though, I quickly stopped by Mather—a long, low-slung dorm at the newer end of campus—to drop my gear in the triple I'd be sharing with two sophomores, Josh Kumpf and David Mastrangelo, who'd pretty much failed the housing lottery. Kenyon has no off-campus housing and so everybody vies for rooms by entering a lottery. There's a separate one for seniors, and back when I was at Kenyon, students in frats got to live in some of the choicest housing at the older end of campus. These days everything is up for grabs, but the students who'd agreed to board me had obviously not done so well. Although they were sophomores, their room was in the basement on a freshman hall.

Moving quickly and with as much purpose as I could muster so I didn't look like some creepy old guy trying to spy on freshman girls,[3] I found the room but instantly realized there had been a mistake. The space, about the size of a McDonald's bathroom and cluttered with computers, a TV, and an electric guitar and amp, was clearly a single, although there were two beds. I was definitely not meant to stay in there. No matter, after swim practice and my evening writing class, I'd get the room's inhabitants to help me find the correct room.

Mather still smelled exactly as it and its twin dorm, McBride, did twenty years ago—a funky mélange of sweaty socks, hair products, deodorants, perfumes, and a mystery ingredient that brought back many equally disturbing memories of my freshman year: praying to porcelain gods and failing at every attempted all-nighter.

Dazed and confused, I made my way to the pool at the new gym, understatement intended. Calling the school's wet-dream-inspired Olympic-length natatorium a "pool" was like calling the *QE2* a "boat." It had great depth, fat lane lines, and water-sucking gutters—all combining to make it one of the fastest racecourses in the country. And the KAC, the Kenyon Athletic Center, was certainly no ordinary gym. It was a glass-encased modern shrine to the school's past, present, and future athletes that pretty much beat any gymnasium I'd ever seen for beauty, design, and functionality. The thing was so outstanding,

---

3. Stumbling over this word on numerous occasions, I finally asked the female students what they called each other and preferred to be called. The answer, to my surprise, was "girls." If I remember correctly, my classmates preferred being called women.

so brightly lit, I guessed you could see its glow from the International Space Station. I found myself absentmindedly wiping smudges off the nearest handrail. It was that gorgeous.

Up in Jim's office (an adult now, I was determined to call him by his first name), a glassed-in turret that towered over his aquatic domain from the second floor, Coach (but I couldn't), now with shiny pate but still a bear of a man, squeezed me hello. Then, stepping back for a better look, he commented, "You don't look a day over thirty-five." A moment later, as he was on hold on the phone, putting the finishing touches on the day's workout and probably thinking about the third turn of his slowest 500 freestyler's last race, he added, "So you're planning on going faster now than you did in college, Hoddo? Well, your sense of timing was always a bit, um . . . different than everybody else's, wasn't it?"

Coach went on to affectionately roast me before the entire swim team out on the pool deck, recalling conversations verbatim from twenty-two years back, focusing mostly on my senior year. He remembered the name of the girlfriend. He remembered the look on my face when he suggested that I miss all the practices if I couldn't make a proper commitment to the team. Better yet, he remembered the same inspiring words that got me back in the pool fully immersed for the first time ever. He even remembered the almost-fight Jeff Moritz and I had at the end of the lane one day. Coach was, and is, a little scary. You never know what he is going to see, say, or do.

Practice itself is better left unexamined. Not only was the vastness of the pool deck overwhelming with some twenty lanes to swim in, but also the swimmers didn't look anything like we had. Except for a handful of softish-looking distance swimmers, the men were all lean and ripped. Compared to my swimming classmates, they looked like extras from *Flex* magazine. They had MUSCLES and hardly a pinch of body fat. Although the guys in my day had been record-setting fast, only a few had visible muscles. The rest, including me even after a year of lifting weights, looked like bookworms at best. And the women were even more intimidating. They reminded me a little bit of those cheating East German swimmers of the 1970s. Remember them? They were the ones who reset every world record in a very short time and dominatrixed the 1976 Olympics, thanks wholly to steroids. They were thick, tall women that you wouldn't want to come across in a darkened alley. Well, many of these Kenyon ladies were nearly as strong.[4]

They were also very fast. One of their very best swimmers, an Olympian from Australia, had swum just a few tenths slower than my college 50-yard-freestyle time.

4. Something odd happens to women swimmers that doesn't usually happen to women in other sports and definitely not to men. When they lift heavy weights and swim miles and miles a day, they oftentimes look, well, chunky. It bothers them to no end. One of the female swimmers complained to me one morning after practice, "I can lift just as much as Josh, but he ends up having a six-pack and I look like the Pillsbury Doughboy. It's not fair!"

(Women are generally two seconds slower than men in the 50 free.) Suffice it to say that despite the fact that I didn't swim my freshman year due to illness and thus still might have another year of NCAA eligibility, Coach didn't ask me to consider another year at Kenyon after seeing me in the pool. We swam three times the distance of my usual workout and I was relegated to the slowest sprint lane with the women's team.

For the most part, I kept up with the women and one guy in my lane, but I'd been sure to get a lot of sleep the night before, eat a lot of carbs for the two days before coming, and had plenty of fluids. They, on the other hand, had been pulling all-nighters (it was near the end of the semester), eating junk food, and probably loafing, since in just a few days they were heading off for Thanksgiving vacation. Each set and each repeat within a set written on the workout board had different colors next to them, indicating the effort each swimmer was supposed to make. While they were constantly changing their effort and speed, I was on only two settings: all out or quit.

Two hours later—like so many other times since returning to swimming—I could only crawl out of the pool.

Hurrying on hands and knees, I had to pass on the sushi offered at the KAC concession because I didn't have any cash. Who would have ever thought there'd be tasty raw ocean fish served in a gym in Gambier, Ohio? I grabbed a couple slices of pizza at the makeshift dining hall across the street from the athletic center. Upper-class meals are usually served in the century-old Pierce Dining

Hall—a steepled and stained-glass affair cherished by the college—but it was being renovated at the time of my visit. It had been my home away from home while at Kenyon. I had eaten at Pierce, slept in there, studied, drank beers (down in the pub), and even made out there. For me, Pierce was Kenyon. As my luck had it, I was stuck getting this first meal and all the rest at Ernst, a building that was the brand-new building when I was first at Kenyon. The kitchen and dining areas sit in the old basketball court, and swim team memorabilia still hang on the walls outside the pool. Despite the long wooden tables borrowed from the real dining hall, it was a pretty poor stand-in for a dining hall and a dreary example of how colleges can waste a lot of money. Ernst had been a big deal when I was in school, with its fancy new pool and seemingly endless locker rooms. One of its raisons d'être had been to provide equal locker and workout space for women, in a hasty attempt to comply with Title IX. It was considerably ugly and the new KAC was a welcome change. But had it really outlived its usefulness in just twenty-four years? If so, maybe Kenyon wasn't going to be such a nurturing place for me. After all, it'd been nearly twenty-four years since I'd graced its pathways.

Mental note to self: do not make analogies.

As I drove across campus under cover of darkness, I realized I wanted to go home.

I really was thinking this but not because of missing Pierce. I was exhausted and hadn't even taken a single class. This was supposed to be a return to those carefree days when I had no kids, no bills, no anything of responsibility. But day one and I was already spent.

It was time, however, to make a good impression in David Lynn's writing class. Besides being an English professor and chairman of the department, he was also the editor of the *Kenyon Review*. Certainly, by the end of class, after hearing my astute remarks concerning his students' stories, David would be begging to publish a few of my lesser works.

Class was held in the basement of Sunset, an old, frumpy house that serves as the English Department's headquarters. My fellow students were already gathered around the round table. Ah, I thought, this was more like it. If my body wasn't up to being a Kenyon Lord then perhaps my mind was. I'd always wanted to take a writing class while I'd been at Kenyon but had been too chicken — a fear of others' editorial opinions that had been instilled in me at my boarding school.[5] This was my

---

5. I hate to go into this here, but I also want to get it off my chest. My first year at my boarding school, I wrote an article for the school's paper. I don't recall what the topic was, just my editor's response. He was an arrogant jock from Princeton—a day student who was not only a whiz with the lacrosse stick but also a respected wordsmith. Or at least he thought he was. No matter, somebody had put him in charge of handling the work of the kids in first and second form. He took one look at my carefully crafted tale and actually threw it back at me, laughing. "Y'aalllll don't use English much down there in Mizzsippiiii, do y'allllll? We can't print this." And that was it. No chance to rewrite, no explanation of what was wrong. I'd been crying myself to sleep almost every night since school started, completely lost and in

big chance. My fellow writers looked much like Kenyon students of 1984: one was wearing the ubiquitous gray hooded sweatshirt with K-E-N-Y-O-N letters that students apparently still find indispensable; another had a scarf wrapped dashingly around his blue overcoat; and another blinded us with his Day-Glo Hawaiian shirt. Seeing that no one had a cell phone pressed against her ear, I abruptly hung up on my daughter Helen, midsentence.

I was wholly insignificant—an adult in a land run by minors. The only adults who made an impression in their world were teachers and celebrities. Since I wouldn't be grading them and I wasn't on TMZ, I didn't really exist.

We dissected three short stories that evening; each discussion was led by a different student but not the author of the work being discussed. That person had to suck it up and take it. I never could've taken that class while I'd been in college.

I liked two of the stories immensely. One was about the

---

pain from my parents' separation, which had occurred just a few weeks before I'd taken off to school. This just added more knowledge to my sudden understanding that I was a loser. That and my Dorothy Hamill haircut. Obviously, I got over my phobia and learned to handle criticism and editing, but it wasn't until after college. I could send in submissions to magazines by mail and, apparently, getting poorly Xeroxed rejection slips through the postal service was much easier on my ego. I persisted and, these days, I can handle just about anything said to me about my writing. When my wife edits a story and I wail like the kid in seat 12A, I'm just joking around.

dangers of chopping off a puppy's head to impress people at your first punk concert. The other was about the rise and fall of a young man's porn empire. Excited by the work, I found myself piping up during the discussions, not as an unfiltered student might but instead in the manner of the reserved, detached gentleman that I'd become since graduation: "You're so wrong. The narrator's lack of emotion is intentional. Don't you understand anything?" I blurted out.

At 9:45, the end of class, David looked at me as if trying to determine exactly how I had been allowed in. "Um, thanks for your input, Hodding. It was very . . . good of you to get so involved," he said, or something like that. It was hard to hear him over the buzz of discourse still careening through my brain.

Driving (okay, it wasn't a walking campus for me) back to Mather I found myself wondering what life would've been like if only I'd done this back in the eighties — attend class, that is. I might actually be running *Harper's* magazine, instead of trying to convince its editor that I'm funny — as I'd recently failed to do.

Back at the dorm, I knocked and then swung the door open. Two boy-men now occupied the previously vacant room. They both had headphones on — one in front of his computer, the other sitting cross-legged before a TV. They looked at me as if wondering where the pizza was (ah, that was the third type of adult who mattered: the pizza-delivery man). I explained the situation and asked if they knew where I was supposed to be staying.

"Oh, no," Josh said. He was the one closest to the door, at the computer. Did he mean that as in, "Oh, no. We have no idea what you're talking about but you're creeping the hell out of me," or did he mean, "Oh no. You're here!" He had this incredibly blank look on his face and it was hard to read anything beyond, "There's an old man talking to me."

"We just need to put your bed together," he continued. The room that I'd judged a single was actually a triple. His bed was missing the upper bunk, that's all.

He and David, the TV watcher on the bed over by the window, stood up and talked to me in that awkward way teenagers reserve for adults who aren't parents or teachers. We were at a bit of an impasse without their knowing it. I debated between telling them to relax and just treat me like another kid, or letting things linger like this; if I did the latter, then maybe they would be quieter, go to sleep earlier, and treat me with unnecessary respect. I opted for lingering respect because although it was only my first day back, I had already been weighed, measured, and definitely found lacking.

After they'd built my bed and we'd chatted for a few hours about classes, school, the food, etc.,[6] I asked them

---

6. Here's a bit of the etc. Josh: It's amazing what we overhear in here. See the crack in the wall, and under the door? We hear everything. David: Remember when they were all talking about back-door entry in the beginning of the year? I couldn't believe what they were telling each other.

what time they went to sleep. I was on the verge of begging them to turn off the lights. I thought these kids would have been prepped to act uncollegelike around me and go to bed at something that resembled a reasonable hour. What were they doing? Didn't they know I was a swimmer? I had to get my sleep! "Sometime after midnight on an early night, much later otherwise," Josh said.

"It doesn't really matter, though," David added, "because of the screamers."

"The screamers?"

"Yeah. They come through practically every night and scream at odd intervals until two, three in the morning."

"It's a little disturbing," Josh helped. "And that's on weeknights. Weekends you can't really sleep at all."

Around midnight, I dozed off while pretending to read a syllabus. David was reading art history and Josh worked on a poli-sci paper. I don't remember staying up this late to do work—even when I had an exam—but then again, my GPA was probably the square root of theirs. A few hours later, I was awoken by my first scream. It seemed more of an extremely high-pitched, loud moan than a scream, but I didn't bother arguing the point.

The one about an hour after that was more your classic screech.

I'd like to say that this was how my week progressed: I slowly got my bearings and as the days accumulated, I became the student within me. That there was no evidence that I was twenty-some years older than everyone else. That I could match them beer for beer. Comeback for comeback. Lap for lap. But that would be a lie. Each day was a repeat of the first one, except the pain just got worse and worse. However, I did try.

On Tuesday, in fact, I was still fired up about getting a chance to take classes again and found myself lecturing a few swimmers on the importance of attending all their classes and doing the assigned work. They looked at me as if I had stated the most obvious thing. Students today apparently aren't like the way I had been. They take college seriously and see it for what it is, a stepping stone. They go to classes, take notes, and actually study for exams. (Lisa has told me that most people, including her, were like this back when we were in school, too—that I was out of step back then as well.)

The biggest mistake I made that day was lifting weights with the sprinters. For the past few years, I'd been doing the same free weight and sit-up routine that had proved so successful my senior year. I was good at these and could lift more than I had been able to while in college. Coach, of course, had developed a completely new routine improved by many current experts, including Mike Bottom, Gary Hall Jr.'s coach. There were plyometric drills, much heavier weights, more repeats, more sets, and killer abdominal sets performed on an exercise ball. I kept falling off the ball, covering each fall by pretending that I was tying my shoe, fixing my buzz-cut hair, or some other obviously unnecessary task. Of course, I didn't want to appear like a forty-four-year-old weenie, so I chose too much weight for nearly every exercise. I was able to walk out of the gym that day. It was the remaining days of the week when I had to resort to crawling.[7]

On Wednesday, still trying to defy my age, I guess, I did both morning and afternoon swim practices, and I entered an energy deficit that I did not recover from until an entire week had passed. On Thursday, I fell asleep in a poli-sci class—just like the good ol' days—and ignored my own advice about seizing the opportunity of being in college by skipping a couple of classes to finish a take-home exam that I should've done the night before.

The take-home was for Wendy MacLeod (the award-winning playwright) and Jon Tazewell's (a former class-mate) Introduction to Drama class. If you want a really freaky experience, take a course taught by a classmate. You can still see him barfing out the third floor dorm window even as he recites passages from *Waiting for Godot* (all right, that was me doing the vomiting, but you get the point).

I'd like to skip over the experience of taking Reed Browning's (another '84 classmate) printmaking class, not just because he didn't let me make a print, but because he also had the brilliant idea of having me talk to the students while he demonstrated some special technique in a different room. The conversations went okay when they talked about how Reed played tennis like an old man,

---

7. The routine they taught me was and is incredible and I believe it's what has helped me improve as much as I have this last year of swimming. Look in the appendix for a detailed description.

employing junk shots to win games, or when they complained about how bad the food and housing is. (Ha! They didn't know bad. We had bug juice, powdered eggs, and mystery meat. They had fresh omelets every morning, food stations that always include a stir-fry table, an excellent pizza table, and endless salad offerings and special entrees like gyro sandwiches that easily beat my local Greek restaurant's efforts.) Things only turned sour when one girl asked me if I'd gotten the tattoo. What tattoo, I asked? Turned out the current Lords got a Kenyon coat of arms tattoo when they made Nationals. When she asked what we had done, I proudly showed her the groundbreaking earring in my left ear.

"That's pretty lame," she pronounced, and an entire group of them turned away from me.

Luckily, I had Perry Lentz's American Lit class to regain my equilibrium, perhaps soothe my aged soul, and put things in perspective. Perry was a fellow southerner by birth. Not only did I take this same American Lit class from him back in the day, he was partially responsible for my becoming an English major. There was something about the way he derided my spelling of "cannot"—I'd tried "can not"—that challenged me (or was it his near-total disregard for *To Kill a Mockingbird*?) into learning more about the medium I loved so much. He became my faculty adviser and I'd always felt like it was his class that set me on my adult path.

Attending his class really was like stepping back in time. Although he had changed the way he lectured and tested his students, now relying on a popular method from the 1800s called recitation, his class was as reassuring as hearing Elvis Costello sing "Alison" one more time. It was not just that he looked exactly the same as he did twenty years ago or even that he raised both the volume and pitch of his voice in the same manner when making a point that the students had best be paying attention to. It was more what he was talking about in his reassuring southern lilt—Thoreau, transcendentalism, and Melville—that set things straight for me.

Emerson tells us to "measure ourselves against what is true—what is real, the natural world," Perry explained. "Don't be caught up in the economics of social order. Our humanity comes alive when you test it for yourself out there in the natural world. It fulfills the reason and the understanding." Nature stimulates the soul.

"In the woods, too," Emerson wrote in *Nature,* "a man casts off his years, as the snake his slough. . . . In the woods is perpetual youth."

For Melville, it was a wholly different matter. Yes, one needs to test oneself in the natural world, but what you find there is going to be altogether different: it is "chaos bewitched."

Sitting in Perry's class, eyes wide open, I realized going back to Kenyon was a lot like entering nature, and I had to say I sided more with Melville than the rest of those namby-pambies. After a week back in college, as a direct result of measuring myself against what is true and real, I realized that I was not the twenty-one-year-old college student that I'd been telling myself I was for more than twenty years. Nor was I the swimmer I had once been. I had not cast off the years, as Emerson promises, and I seemed to have gained worry lines and bulges that were not there previously. Being there made me see all these wretched truths about myself. For the first time in my adult life, I felt my age: forty-four. I was aware of this fact before I slept in the dorm, took classes, ate in Ernst, swam at the KAC, and walked down Middle Path, but it wasn't etched in my psyche. It wasn't truly who I was because, God knew, I was really only twenty-one—twenty-eight, at the oldest. Now, thanks to all those college women ignoring my longing look and being trounced in the pool, I knew myself. I may even have grown up.

Nine

It's an Honor, Mr. Carter

I didn't realize this at the time, but this swimming thing, this attempt to beat the odds of my middle age, was turning out to be a mental puzzle. As time went on, more and more pieces were falling into place. Not everything was immediately clear but I was making the right moves, turning the pieces in the right direction to solve my aquatic puzzle. The only question was time. Would I have enough to put it all together?

At least I knew I was on the right track with the sprinting thing. I was in decent shape when I went back to Kenyon for my triumphant return, yet I could barely keep up with the slowest sprinters in practice. When we did sprint relays one day, however, I could beat all the women, and most of the guys.

The nice thing about this confirmation was that I could stop doing so much yardage. I was free to focus on gaining more strength to the detriment of everything else, including my aerobic conditioning. Unless a person has spent hour after hour, day after day, following that annoying black line up and down, back and forth, in and out of turns, it is almost impossible to comprehend the joy I felt. A great weight had been lifted from my aged shoulders. I no longer had to practice sustaining 180 heartbeats per minute for ten to fifteen minutes at a time, or even 160 for thirty—those exhausting rates that divide the old from the young, the sprinter from the distance athlete—day after day. I would still have to hit those ranges and higher but for much shorter intervals and infrequently. In other words, I would have to try harder in practice but for much shorter periods—like say, ten seconds versus ten minutes.

Why hadn't I thought of this before?

The 50 had been my worst race at Nationals—I'd placed only twelfth or something like that. I'd been less than a second off Olympic Trial cuts back then, but in the 50, that was a lot of time. But it definitely represented my current best chance. I was only down to a 22.4 in the 50-yard free. To make Olympic Trials, I needed to be swimming a 20.4 or so—a good two seconds faster. However, that 20.4 was "only" 1.2 seconds off my best time from college. All of this is confusing but what it meant after many complicated calculations and rationalizations was that I'd finally found the race that I had half a chance at qualifying for, but it was going to take a lot of concentrated training.

I wrote Coach, asking if my new approach made sense. I hadn't been able to talk with him beyond the first day because his brother's condition worsened and he'd left Kenyon while I was visiting (in fact, his brother died a few weeks later and Coach wrote a heartfelt eulogy that brought me to tears). I almost but didn't quite admit what my goal was. I only said that I wanted to go faster than I had in college and did he think it was possible? His answer surprised the hell out of me and once again made me cry. Maybe it was just that time of the month or maybe it was having somebody who knew the situation believe in me.

He wrote back, "Can you swim faster in the 50 (21.6, I believe) than you did at Kenyon? I'm sure you can! If you train efficiently and correctly. If I was training for the 50, you can bet your bottom dollar I wouldn't be wasting any time on aerobic training beyond warming up! . . . I'm sending you a couple sets of workouts that might give you a few ideas. What is your timetable for swimming this awesome 50? Where are you planning on doing it? Have you generated a plan (beyond the further wet dreams of Hodding Carter)?"

Well, at least I knew he really had been upset by that Mark Spitz article. He went on to outline what I should do, what supplements I needed (creatine, multis, etc.), suggested I not waste my time with aerobic conditioning, and sent me some sample workouts. His e-mail became my bible or at the very least my blueprint for the entire following year.

Meanwhile, at home, Lisa and I fell into a more comfortable rhythm. We'd wake up, rush through the house waking children, making cheese grits, packing lunches, waking children again, and loading them into separate cars. She'd take Angus and Helen to childcare and elementary school, respectively, and I'd rush the twins off to middle school. Then, during the school day, she'd cram lawyering between errands and school functions and I'd juggle lifting, swimming, and writing with taking Angus to yet another appointment to get tubes in his ears or have Helen dewormed. We'd reunite when school was over, stuff food into their gaping mouths—wishing we could just regurgitate our food like some of those birds you see on nature shows—and then rush them off to the Y (my third visit for the day, probably) so they could practice hip-hop dancing and then do swim team practice. All three girls were on the team, although I swore I hadn't influenced them. We'd come back home at 7:45, whip up enough calories so they wouldn't look like famine victims, which they were always on the verge of resembling, and then pass out by nine p.m.

With the exception of my warm-up and recovery days, practically everything I did was fast and short, both in real life and in the water. I stopped swimming entire lengths of the pool and instead focused on twelve-and-a-half-yard sprints with lots of rest. I also went absolutely crazy on the weights, and within a very short time I'd gained more than ten pounds of muscle, bettering my college gains. It was an eerie transformation and one that had Mike Schmidt suggesting at the New England Local Masters

Swimming Committee Short Course Meter Champion-ships (now that's a mouthful) that I'd been taking HGH. I was buff.

One day, Lisa walked into our bedroom with a load of laundry towering three feet over her head. "Could you get that for me?" she said.

"What?" I answered guiltily. I was bent over, shirtless, flexing my muscles. I'd been doing it for at least fifteen minutes, the entire time she'd been folding *our* clothes.

A sock had dropped by my feet. I picked it up, handed it to her, and unthinkingly, went back to admiring myself.

"Nice," she said. I was so infatuated that I thought she was serious.

"Thanks," I answered, a huge smile stretching across my . . . wait, it couldn't be . . . wrinkled face.

Maybe it was my mirror time or just all the muscles and focused sprint training but something made me a little bit faster. Although it had been only six weeks or so, I set the New England record for the 50-meter free-style short course at the championships that December. I was the laughingstock of the Maine Masters contingency, however, because unlike everyone else, who made up for leaving their families and work to race in skimpy suits by competing in eight to ten races over the course of the two-day meet, I drove all the way down there just to race the 50. Mike Schmidt had come up to me a couple of times and asked, "Are you okay?" which, at the time, I thought was a very sweet gesture since, in good masters fashion, I wasn't feeling in tip-top form (remember, we had to have our excuses). It wasn't until much later that I realized he had probably been ribbing me, suggesting I must be looney for traveling so far for a twenty-four-second race.

As the winter wore on, I continued to train as Coach had directed me. In fact, I definitely went overboard in the nonaerobic side of things and limited slow swimming to such a degree that I was winded even when I did endurance maintenance sets. Most of my training centered around this device I bought from Coach called the Power Rack. It's a simple but ingenious device that lets a swimmer do resistance training with increasable weights while swimming. It is the best way to look like a total dork at your local Y and gain explosive strength at the same time. With the rack, I could lift up to one hundred pounds while swimming by sprinting on a tether attached to a Nautilus-like weight-lifting machine placed at the end of the pool. Its only drawback is that a swimmer can only go eleven and a half yards before the weights reach the top of the rack and the sprint is over.

As the New England Masters Short Course Yards Championships approached, I decided to meld the kids' swimming and mine by competing alongside them at the Maine winter championships. The only problem was, they didn't qualify. They swam at their Y state meet but the age-group championships were a bit more competitive. So, like their father when it came to the Olympic Trials qualifying times, they didn't make the cut times. I did, however, and since I'd also told a few of the older swimmers on their team that I'd do a relay with them, we went to the meet in March.

What I remember most from that meet was a constant low-level embarrassment—the kind you get when your dad stands up in a crowded restaurant and starts reciting some poem he'd memorized as a child (yeah, that's happened to me), except, in this case, I was the dad. I'd always been comfortable walking around in my Speedo as a kid and even recently at masters meets—we were oblivious to how we might look—but most young swimmers today don't wear skimpy Speedos when they race. They wear these long, extremely tight shorts called jammers, or they cough up lots of dough and wear tech suits. I'd decided not to wear mine—I didn't want to look too desperate—so I'd brought my skimpy Speedo.

Here was the difference between being a twenty-five-year-old Olympic hopeful and a forty-five-year-old Olympic wannabe: The twenty-five-year-old strips down to his suit and feels lost in the crowd. Every time I took off my shorts, I felt like the thousand parents in the stands and all their children milling around the Bowdoin College pool deck were staring at me. It was worse than one of those caught-in-your-underwear-in-high-school dreams. Eventually, I took to wearing my jeans and T-shirt until I was just behind the block, and then right before they called my heat, I slipped out of my clothes quickly, like an eager virgin.

Even so, I swam fairly well, especially considering it was the first weekend of my official taper for New Englands. The biggest mistake I made was racing the 100 butterfly.

I looked over at Will Guinther, the eighteen-year-old kid from my Y who would be entering West Point in less than half a year. He was going for a 52—much faster than my goal for the day. Lo and behold, I was ahead at the 50. Oh yeah. A second later, though, I regretted turning my neck while swimming so hard as it sort of stuck in that sideways glance due to the arthritis I had from breaking my neck fifteen years back. A few more seconds along, however, and it didn't really matter. By that point, my amateurish mistake of starting the race too fast—going out hard, as we say—caught up to me. First, the guy to my immediate right slipped past, and then, as it appeared that somebody had tied some weights to my arms, Will inched even with me. By the time we reached the third turn, I wondered why nobody had called the police. Obviously, some evil villain had either stabbed me with a hundred knives or, at the very least, dropped a searingly hot anvil across my back.

Would it be okay, I wondered, if I just hung onto the wall and didn't swim the last lap? Nobody would notice if I stayed submerged with only my lips breaking the surface, my defeated body hidden beneath the roughened waters. Would I be able to last until everybody left and they shut off the lights?

I tried to push off for the last lap. I got off the wall but

I wouldn't really call it a push. I would have had to have working legs, and by that point they'd gone from death-desiring pain to complete numbness. Oddly, Will and the other heat leaders were only a few feet ahead of me. If I could just . . . manage . . . to . . . bring . . . both . . . arms . . . out . . . of . . . the . . . w . . . a . . . t . . . e . . . r . . . . There! I did it. Now I had only eight more of those to go. Go, Hodding, go. Try as I did, they wouldn't cooperate beyond exiting the water together and entering together out front. I managed to stay legal, but those who were ahead, stayed ahead, and everyone else began to pass me by.

Not every race went that poorly, of course. I made it to finals in all my races and took fifth or sixth among all those fifteen- to twenty-one-year-olds in the 50. Afterward, as I hobbled back to my team's sitting area, a boy who looked like he might have been born around the time I got my first gray hair, grabbed my hand. "It's an honor to be racing against you, Mr. Carter," he said. Had his parents paid him to say this? I couldn't decide whether or not I should feel good or bad from the comment. Of course, it made me feel old but I like to think he thought I was pretty fast for an old fart. I decided it was a good thing.

I was turning over a new leaf in my swimming life. At first I couldn't put my finger on it but at New Englands the following weekend when Bill Rupert and I roomed together again and we joked about how we could finally have some fun since Mike Schmidt wasn't around to curtail our spending and I almost took a swig out of the plastic cup that held Bill's false teeth, I realized that I belonged to something. The warm and fuzzy thing about it was that it wasn't the kind of thing most adults belong to. It wasn't based on wealth or success. It didn't require paying dues beyond the yearly fifty-dollar membership. It just took showing up and hanging out, talking about things and farting in each other's faces. When Bill, Andy and his family, a few others, and I all went to Chris Schlesinger's East Coast Grill in Somerville, I realized that the loud, bubbly conversation adding to the restaurant's deafening acoustics was coming from our table. It was an effortless comfortable sound — just like what you might hear when hanging around a . . . swim team. Boy, did it sound good.

In the pool, things weren't so bad either. I won the 50 free and the 50 fly (surprise), posting 22.3 and 24.4, respectively.

A few weeks later, I drove down to Virginia with Mike Schmidt, Bill Rupert, Mike Ross, and Beth Fries to race in the masters sectional meet. It was supposed to be the championships for everybody from Florida to Maine, but it depends on the year if it really represents such a wide-ranging championship. Recently, it'd been held at George Mason University, which has a very fast pool, so any regional masters swimmer on a mission would usually show up.

Mike, Bill, Mike, and Beth had become a band of swimmers the last few years, driving to and flying to and sleeping together at many of the big meets around the country. I was their new member. Mike Ross, thirty-nine at the time, was and is the reigning god of New England masters swimming. He'd been a champion swimmer at Princeton in the late 1980s and had swum even better after graduating from there, qualifying for a total of three Olympic Trials. His last was in 2000, at the age of thirty-two. Since then, he had broken practically every national masters record in the races he'd swum and, unlike me, looked like he could make the 2008 Trials if he focused himself well enough. I'd been aiming to beat him for about a year but hanging out together was probably more rewarding—and likely.

Beth, forty-nine, was a nurse practitioner from Keene, New Hampshire, and Mike Schmidt's main disciple. She wasn't a fast swimmer but her freestyle stroke kept getting better and better. More importantly, she was a wonderful companion, egging us on to talk about our sex lives, bowel movements, and even our feelings. When Beth was around, one of us would ask, "Beth, so what does it mean when a woman says. . . ." I still haven't figured out what we did for her in return.

I didn't know either Mike Ross or Beth very well at the beginning of the drive but after a few hours of revealing truths and after the conversation about the best positions one should assume for making babies, I felt like we'd all been buddies for a very long time. Compared to our conversations, the meet itself was fairly tame, except that I went even faster than I had at New Englands, getting a 22.2 in the 50.

I was now within 0.55 seconds of my best 50 ever.

Just as I'd hoped and planned, I was doing what most elite masters swimmers considered impossible.[1] I was getting faster even as I was getting older. The only problem was that I was running out of time. It'd taken me an entire year to drop just two-tenths off my 50. How was I going to drop another 1.7 in time?

Get a job.

---

1. People new to the sport improve their times quite often the first few years, even though they're getting older, because their technique makes such drastic improvements. Of course, if everybody was thinking my way, even the elite swimmers who had time for serious training would continue to make gains but, alas, the revolution hasn't yet begun.

Ten

Swim, Forrest, Swim!

Before heading off to Las Vegas to reclaim his own youth, Jason Amos, the twenty-two-year-old assistant aquatics director and head swim coach at my Y, sucker punched me—and badly, although I am speaking metaphorically. If I remember correctly, sometime in February 2006, he started complimenting my swimming at every lap. At first, it was fairly innocent things like, "Wow, Hodding, that was a fast twelve and a half" or "Man, I wish I could go that fast" or "You're definitely going to Beijing." I smiled and took it all at face value. After all, I was wicked fast, right? Then, he started saying how good I was with the swim team kids and how glad he was that I was around to help out when he needed it.

Did I think something was up? No. I just appreciated him noticing the obvious.

I didn't catch on that he'd been buttering me up for the roasting until sometime in early March. Just before

New Englands, he asked if I wanted to be the swim coach starting next month. Me, the man who hadn't had a real job in fifteen years, work for somebody? It would mean responsibility, coming to the Y every day for more than just my workouts, anxious and/or aggressive parents, fickle kids (or worse, uncaring ones), and anxiety, lots of anxiety. Why would I want to take this on?

The problem was that all this swimming combined with the marital problems Lisa and I had experienced the previous year had put us into a deep, deep monetary hole. I'd written all sorts of articles the past year to help lift us out, but that hadn't erased our financial woes. Lisa had been working full-time at a local law practice, but that hadn't worked out since they were keeping more of her hourly earnings than she. She decided to start her own firm and work from home.

I needed to make a bold move, too. Why not coach and apply for the aquatics director job? Jason was the co-aquatics director along with a woman who'd just graduated from college. The only reason why he wasn't the aquatics director was because he hadn't graduated from college. It looked like, when he left, the aquatics director position would need filling.

I typed up my first résumé in sixteen years and applied for the job. I hadn't worked for anybody since 1992, and I'd never run a department of any kind. Hell, for that matter, even my aquatics credentials didn't look all that sharp—at least on paper. I'd been a lifeguard only one summer and my coaching had been limited to helping out with my home team in Mississippi when I was a teenager, working as a counselor and lane coach for Coach Steen at his swim camp after graduating from college, and coaching a swim team in Africa during my Peace Corps stint. Coaching in Africa admittedly was a bit of a joke, although it looked good on a résumé. I taught lessons, but most of my time was spent literally scooping kids off the bottom of the pool. No matter how long I had them practice floating in the shallow end, every time I'd take them to the deep, they would sink. I honestly dove down and brought up more than one hundred children in a single season.

Regardless, I got the job, although not as director, but as assistant director. It provided my family with medical insurance, a steady income, and free membership. And it also provided a venue for testing and teaching my newly formed swimming theories. All of those reasons amounted to a good thing but the real reason I took it was for my own swimming. I'd be able to swim almost whenever I wanted. I could always jump in and try out techniques. Plus, immersing myself in the aquatics world seemed like the right thing to do. Everything was going to click. I just knew it.

At first, though, the only thing that really clicked was my sanity. It clicked off. I had never done anything as difficult as this job for such a long period of time. My hat was suddenly off to all those overlooked and underappreciated aquatics workers throughout the world. Being a teacher and not just a director does have its rewards—there's nothing much better than the feeling you get when you teach a kid to swim—but that didn't really make up for everything else. At all the Ys I've been acquainted with over the years (and there have been quite a few, starting with my hometown Y in Greenville, Mississippi) the aquatic director's position has had the most turnover. We had ten people as director and assistant director in the nine years I'd lived here, and suddenly, I realized, for good reason. A year ago, I had not a single gray hair; now they were all over the place.

I was right about having more chances to swim, but luckily, I'd decided to race the 50, because the chances were always for short periods—maybe forty-five minutes at the very most. Between swiveling my hips with a class of sixty-year-olds during Liquid Toning class and filling out time sheets for the lifeguard staff, I could sneak in a warm-up and a handful of repeats with the Power Rack. It was great training for any race that might last six seconds but not so good for something a little longer, like, for instance, swimming around Manhattan.

How I wish that was a mere example and not the very next big swim on my horizon, but wishes don't always come true. On the warm cloudless morning of June 16, 2007, I found myself standing on Pier 11 anxiously awaiting a chance to swallow a mouthful or two of New York City's world-class sewage.

To be fair, the chance of swallowing outright raw sewage was next to none, thank God, because it hadn't rained for days. I'd literally been praying for months that it wouldn't rain. Okay, actually, I'd been praying for months that it would rain because if it did, the annual Manhattan Island Marathon Swim organizers would have had to cancel the outing because the city's drainage system is so antiquated.

In the old days, meaning anytime before the 1972 Clean Water Act, city planners didn't have to concern themselves with the water quality of run off as long as it dumped into a body of water that flowed away from the city being planned. So, in the late 1800s, when New York City's planners were designing and building the separate subterranean canals that carry runoff water and sewage, respectively, they could prepare for handling the surge from huge storms by allowing the storm waters to spill over into the sewage canals. It was far simpler and more cost effective than building yet another canal beneath the city's streets that would be used only perhaps a dozen times a year. This is how they did it the world over for centuries, and it's one of the many reasons why our urban waterways were so frightening for so long.

Many forward-looking cities, a list that includes places like Boston and London but not New York, have straightened their backs in recent years and done the right thing, spending billions on improving their sewage systems. Even when it rains like Noah's business, the two waters do not intermix in those cities. But New York is not one of those places. When a deluge descends, the relatively clean street water streams down to the underground canals, overflows into all that toilet water from all those fancy buildings, and dumps right into the city's moat.[1] That's how you get storm water fish kills and that's what I had been vainly begging for. If the bacteria count was high enough, they'd cancel the swim. This morning, however, as I pulled my minivan into the unsurprisingly vacant parking lot at five a.m., the rivers and tidal canals surrounding Manhattan were at their finest. The swim was on.

I'd been flattered when Alan Schmidt had asked me to join his relay team back in September. Alan, some kind of marketing guy in New York, had graduated from Kenyon more than four years after me. Our paths had crossed when I returned from the Peace Corps and swum at Kenyon for a month while searching for a place to train for that period's attempt at Olympic immortality. Alan and I spoke only a few times during that brief return to Gambier, Ohio, but something about the way I traded punches with George Pond had impressed Alan.[2] Or maybe Alan had seen the story I'd written about that swim I took in

1. In that respect, the waters surrounding Manhattan are much like ye moats of olde. Those fairytale waters of splendor so serenely illustrated in childrens' stories were disgusting, E. coli–breeding cesspits, festering with bedpan leavings, bloated carcasses, and anything else that helped make them such perfect deterrents to invasion. If the drawbridge was raised, only the bravest of knights wanted to wade those watery wastelands.

2. George was supposed to be a senior but had had some difficulties since my graduation; I'd been his mentor of sorts and had obviously led him astray. Perhaps teaching him the best technique for handling a beer bong hadn't been so bright after all.

the British Virgin Islands and so he knew that, unlike many of our fellow Kenyon alums, I was currently aware of the sensation of water swirling past my body due to my own exertions. Or perhaps he was testing my claims to Olympic greatness. The few people who'd noticed that I was claiming I was going to qualify for the Trials were nearly all ex-Kenyon swimmers. I think I was some kind of embarrassment for them. I'd heard there was a hit out on me, even, but that was said by the same guy who had, during college, stared at me from across one of the Pierce Hall dining tables one evening and said, "I don't know why anybody ever goes out with you. You're as skinny as a twig but you have a double chin." I don't think he always had my best interest at heart.

Whatever the reason, when Alan originally asked me to do the swim, it was easy to commit. I had just returned from Worlds, a reinvigorated swimmer willing to take on anything. I'd been doing some endurance base work and had just won a three-and-a-half-mile race in sixty-degree water (with a racing wet suit). I had been befuddled, having momentarily taken on the role of Super Swimmer. Also, it was six months away. Of course I could handle it. The total distance was 28 miles. Divided by six swimmers, we'd each swim about 4.7 miles, most of it with a current. I could do it backstroke and still beat most people.

But that had been before I'd converted to only sprint training, *and* before I learned I wouldn't be able to wear a wet suit. The Manhattan swim would demand two forty-five-minute legs without a wet suit—English Channel rules—for each of us in the relay. The very fact that the organizers and fellow competitors were bandying about such words as "English Channel rules" should have been an obvious "whoa," but at the time, many months away, it had seemed so far off, and even when I had come to my senses and given up all distance swimming for good, I remembered it was a swim, after all, not a race. I could go as slowly as I wanted.

"I'm not sure we're going to win this thing," Alan nearly whispered conspiratorially as he and I stood just inches apart, then he motioned eastward toward a bunch of goons standing at the edge of the pier. "Those dudes came from Australia, and George has, um, tapered a bit too much. He hasn't swum in weeks."

I looked at him directly for the first time ever. He had to be joking. Win? But his face didn't reveal what I was hoping. Instead, what I saw atop this super-lean, extremely fit forty-year-old's body (he'd just taken off his shirt for a photographer from *New York* magazine) was a look of such determination and worry that I found myself really, really wishing I hadn't driven through the night, swilling a quart of coffee and singing "Free Falling" desperately out of tune, over and over again.

"This is a race?" I asked. "They call it a swim on the Web site. You're not planning on swimming fast, are you?"

"Ha, ha. Very funny, Hoddo." He wasn't smiling, and by this point, neither was I.

I'm not sure what I'd been thinking, but I hadn't ever

considered that we were swimming to win or go fast. We had all been trading e-mails for months, ribbing each other, joking about what kind of shape we were in, and vying for the last leg of the relay. Dennis Mulvihill, a six-eight loudmouthed lawyer from Michigan (and perhaps the most accomplished swimmer in our bunch, having swum fast enough to qualify for the Olympic Trials in the 200 and 500 frees during his college years), had figured out that although we'd have to swim through the lineup twice, the last swimmer might only have to swim once. Winners in the past had finished in less than seven and a half hours. Since there were six of us and we each had to swim forty-five minutes, if all went well (meaning we were anywhere near eight hours), we'd be at the finish line even before the fifth swimmer on our relay finished his second leg. If all went well.

Judging by the morning's events thus far, that "if" seemed very unlikely. Earlier, at 5:55 a.m., to be precise, I'd been standing under FDR Drive just south of South Street Seaport, nodding off while standing, when I saw Alan and Elliot Rushton, our twenty-three-year-old ringer, exit from a cab. Although the blondish curls I remembered had given way to a mostly hairless dome, I was happy that I even recognized Alan. There were a lot more fools standing under the roadway waiting for the beginning of the race than I'd imagined there would be — some eighty-seven swimmers would be competing, twenty-five of whom were swimming it all by themselves.

Anyway, as I was saying hello, Alan spun around, head followed closely by body, whirling around in the universal sign for, *Where the hell is my . . . ?*

"They're in the cab!" he yelled. "My camera and all my gear. Stop!" But the driver was far out of earshot. So, for the next half hour, while he should have been jaw boning and ribbing the rest of us for being wholly unprepared for swimming forty-five minutes straight in sixty-seven- to sixty-eight-degree water, he was mostly busy trying to track down his ten thousand dollars' worth of gear, most of which was borrowed. (He never found it.) Personally, I would've used the whole incident as a perfect excuse to swim slowly (and really wished he had) or skip the whole thing entirely, but as soon as the rest of the motley crew had shown up, he had all but put it behind him.

The motley crew, of course, wasn't so motley—or at least there had been a point in each of our lives when we hadn't been. There was: Alan—eighteen-time All-America[3] swimmer. He was our leader. It was his idea to enter the race and he was the only one of us who actually lived in New York. Dennis Mulvihill, the big guy. He was currently a fairly big-time lawyer operating out of Hudson, Ohio. I'm not sure how big-time he was except for the fact that he'd just been working on a case down in Miami. George Pond, the only other sprinter in the group (and thus it was us against them for the entire day until

3. To be an NCAA All-America swimmer means you finish in the top six at nationals.

he, too, turned on me). George is a landscape architect and is the director of something having to do with that at the Denver museum. Karel Starek, the fittest of the bunch. Karel had lost all his hair and looked like a short, mottled Mr. Clean. Okay, he looked nothing like the cartoon character except for being bald and fit. Karel was in a midcareer transition, he and his wife having just sold their business. The instant I saw him it warmed my heart. We'd been buddies at Kenyon although he was two years my junior, and I swore we'd now stay in touch (we didn't). Karel, perhaps slightly less accomplished back in college than the other guys, was the only one of us in decent distance-swimming shape. Elliot Rushton, twenty-three, our ringer. He took twelfth at the 2005 Open Water World Championships. He won the mile at NCAA Division III Nationals in 2005 and still held the record in it. Elliot was helping out with the team when I spent my week at Kenyon the previous fall and worked in the athletic center as the assistant building coordinator for technology, whatever that meant.

With Elliot, Dennis, and Alan on the team, it seemed like we couldn't lose, despite Alan's worries and the fact that I'd stayed up all night to drive down to New York from Maine. Standing on the boardwalk, waiting for our boat to pick us up, I, at least, thought we were going to win.

Except, it didn't quite go that way, and the unpleasant and unforeseen turn of events, regrettably, had everything to do with me.

Things were fine at first, besides Alan's camera fiasco. Everyone showed up. We picked up our goody bags, which had a cheap pen and notepad and a swim cap, which we had to write our number on. Conversations flowed. We all knew each other, except for Elliot, but he had easily integrated. He was, quite recently, what we had once been—a national champion—and so all the guys were eager to accept him. Also, they'd all eaten dinner together the night before, so I was the only one feeling a little bit disconnected. It certainly didn't help any that I hadn't slept all night. As we stood there, waiting for our boat to arrive, I wondered why I'd thought driving all night was such a bright idea. True, I hadn't wanted the event to cost any more money. Entry fees were more than $1,200 total. But it had also been out of cockiness. I thought I was the only one in halfway decent shape, besides Elliot. I didn't need sleep to do as well as these old farts (not including Elliot, we were all over forty, although I was the oldest). And a little voice was telling me I'd been able to do this kind of thing in college so why not now if I was such a hotshot athlete? No matter what my thinking had been, I suddenly realized how stupid I'd been as I nodded off while talking to Karel. I mean, Karel was boring and all, but not that boring.

A few minutes later, after I'd made my excuses and Alan had found out about my no-doze night, he freaked out a little. "You did what? Why on earth would you do such a thing? . . . You're okay, though, right? It's just like pulling an all-nighter, that's all."

Considering the look of relief that crossed his face when he reassured himself, I chose not to tell him that I had never pulled an all-nighter during my entire college career.

Soon, Elliot went off with the other first swimmers on a bus to the other side of lower Manhattan, Battery Park City. That's where the race would start and finish. Pier 11, just below South Street Seaport, was the point of embarkation for the relay members. The way the relay would work was that one swimmer did a forty-five-minute leg. The rest of us would ride in a boat and then, a few minutes before the swimmer's leg was over, the next swimmer would jump in and begin swimming. For the transition to be legal, the swimmer being replaced had to be in front of the new swimmer when the time was up. Each boat had a volunteer judge, or code enforcer, if you will, to ensure this was done properly.

The only other person who looked as nervous as I felt was George. Although he'd started his career at Kenyon as a distance swimmer and had been the national champ in the mile his freshman year, he'd converted to sprinting by his junior year. Although he'd tried to get some yardage in the past few months, he was as unprepared for swimming distance as I was.

And we were all scared of the cold, except for Alan, who'd already done a few races in the Hudson. The water temperature, sixty-seven degrees, was low enough to induce hypothermia within forty-five minutes if the swimmer wasn't generating enough of his own heat. Since we were swimming fairly hard, hypothetically we'd not have any problems maintaining our core temperature. Hypothetically.

When we finally embarked on our boat, a private fishing yacht captained and crewed by volunteers, and the temperature climbed into the low seventies and nary a cloud could be seen, I found myself thinking it could be worse — it could be the 1980s. Back then, local toughs would drop bricks or whatever they could get their hands on from bridges when swimmers unknowingly entered their territory.

In the first half-hour, as everyone except Elliot lounged in the boat's stern, waiting for our leg of the race, I was talking pretty big, explaining to the captain that we had to head out away from shore around certain bends to escape the eddies that ran counter to the current we were riding. Although we were going counterclockwise around the city and thus up the East River, the ocean tides dominated and a three- to four-knot current carried us north. I explained to the guys that they needed to "ferry" across a current — swim upstream at an angle — rather than try to swim directly across. I also took the opportunity to boast about my past river-running experiences, leaving out any account about the passengers I flipped out of my boat by accident.

I did all these things because I was high on caffeine and no sleep, and soon, very soon, I was wishing I'd kept my big mouth shut.

When Elliot came into view in first place, I wanted to scream with frustration and anger. I'd been hoping his record had all been bravado—inflated through the Internet perhaps. But he was the real deal. There were people from all around the world—literally, the second-place finisher of the entire race was a woman from Australia—but he was kicking their collective ass. Instead of screaming obscenities like I wanted to, I played along with Alan and the others and cheered wildly. "Go, Elliot. Yea! You're the man! Take that, you lousy Aussie! We're the Lords!"

There was no way I could maintain the lead.

Maybe I could poison him.

Luckily, Alan, Karel, and Dennis were before me. Surely one of them would lose it, taking the pressure off me. The only good thing was that by the time Elliot's leg was over—about ten minutes later—he'd gone on the outer edge of the current. We were in third when Alan dove in, just past the Brooklyn Bridge.

I'd like to say I marveled at the wonders of the bridge and learned oh-so-much more about the city from this river-rat-eye's view, but it wasn't so. For the most part, I noticed only one thing: my fear.

Alan kept us in third. Dennis did the same. Then Karel, the hairless punk, dove in.

"Karel's looking good," Alan said a few minutes later. There was an air of hope in his voice, a note that'd been missing all morning, probably because of the camera thing but more likely because the harsh realities of his relay squad had momentarily taken the wind out of him. We all looked out across the water and it was true, Karel, the traitor, was looking mighty good.

"That a boy, Karel!" Dennis screamed, taking up the banner. The others chimed in and soon we were the Lords once again. I was surprised when nobody broke out with the Kenyon clap. Seemingly feeding off our cheers, Karel proceeded to pick off the race leaders one by one. By the time I jumped in on the Harlem River, we were in the lead, not by much, but we were in the lead. Tellingly, the tide had gone completely slack.

"You can do it, Hoddo," George screamed at me just before my head went underwater. I glanced back to catch his smirk, appreciating the inside joke. At least he wasn't taking this too seriously. But there he was, leaning over the gunwale, a determined expression in place of the expected goofy grin. He even gave me a thumbs up.

Jesus.

For the first minute or so, things went well. I even noticed how briny the water was. Hmmm, how interesting. Since we were way up in Harlem, I'd been expecting fresh, not salt, water but of course we were in the tidal zone. While it was decidedly café au lait brown, it smelled and felt clean. The whole time I was cognizant, I didn't see a single bit of trash, just the occasional stick of wood. In fact, none of us would come across anything worse than a couple of balloons and one distended, evidently used condom. Gone were the days when swimmers ran into couches, refrigerators, and dead people.[4]

---

4. Happily, none of us ended up sick after the race was over either—even weeks later when nasty conditions like giardia would usually show up. Considering that if you even fell into one of the city's

So, at first, things were fine. But soon I began to regret not only going without sleep the night before, drinking the dozen cups of coffee, and taking the caffeine pills I'd been offered thirty minutes earlier, but also my entire life. What was I but an exceptionally large molecule that loved Jimmy Swaggart, and what was that car-sized barracuda doing with my left foot? No matter, I didn't have a body, did I? He could have it for his museum.

Yes, that's really how I was thinking. Something very, very bad had happened to my brain from the cold and lack of sleep and perhaps the caffeine. At first, I simply hadn't been able to feel my hands and feet. Then my stomach turned cold, like it was wrapped in an ice blanket. My arms felt like somebody else was controlling them. I also felt shame. Man, had I not held up my end of things. About ten minutes into my leg, I felt like I was actually going to drown and for this small favor, I felt thankful. I'd never felt this way my entire life, and I'd always laughed at Lisa for worrying about my thinking I was invincible in the water. But it was true: I couldn't swim my way out of everything. Clearly, I was going down.

I stopped swimming and looked over at the guys in the boat. Surely they could see the horror on my face. That I had to be pulled out. That no race was worth my life.

Ah, thank God, they were motioning to me, saying

---

rivers back in the early seventies you might end up dying, things had improved dramatically. If the city would revamp its sewage and drainage system, the New York waterways would probably have a full recovery.

something that I couldn't make out. I put a hand to my ear.

"Swim, Hoddo, swim!"

"Get going, Hodding!"

Even our safety kayaker joined in. "Swim. Come on, you can do it," she called. The wretch. She was the closest to me. She was nearly on my level and only a few feet away. She was clearly a Nazi.

Somehow I swam on. Eventually, I completely lost my mind and I didn't even know or care how badly I was doing. Somehow I left my body although I sensed others passing me. I had no idea how many or by how much. By the time I came up for air and back to the real world, we were in fifth place and the lead seemed to be nearly a half-mile ahead.

I had to be pulled over the gunwale from the diving platform. I couldn't make my hands and legs cooperate. It took more than thirty minutes for the shaking to go away. Karel asked if I wanted to see a doctor. Dennis and Alan huddled a few feet away and words like "medevac" and "blew the lead" and "worried" drifted toward me as I slumped there, shaking and wishing I had just said no.

They decided I shouldn't swim again since I obviously couldn't handle the cold and I readily agreed. And that probably would have been that, except there was nowhere for me to go. I was stuck on the boat. I watched George catch us back up a bit to third. Then Elliot got back in around the Hudson and surprisingly didn't catch up to the two leaders. In the first and second spot then were a

four-man team from New York and a solo woman from
Australia. She was forty-four years old and shorter than
any of us, yet only Karel was able to swim faster than she
could. Alan didn't gain on her and Dennis appeared to
lose a bit of ground to her. George, who was supposed to
go after me, took my place and held ground, so to speak,
but we were still a good three to five minutes behind.

Elliot was getting ready to get in for a third time when
I told him I'd swim.

"I don't think that's a good idea, Hodding," Dennis
said, and everybody joined in. I couldn't tell if they were
more concerned for my health or about getting farther
behind, but I now had something to prove.

When I dove in, we were somewhere along midtown,
and I had a good five miles to go. Judging by my last swim,
Elliot would probably have to swim one more time even if
I completed my leg. But that wasn't how it happened.

I don't know if it was the caffeine pills wearing off
or some kind of metabolic change induced by my mild
hypothermia, but I swam much faster the second time
around. I even gained a bit on the Australian woman.
Now that I was feeling more like myself, I was surprised that I couldn't beat her, but then I remembered
the race director cautioning Alan about having victori-
ous expectations. The experienced open-water, long-
distance swimmers could kick our pool-swimming asses
any day. The previous year, the former Olympic great
Jenny Thompson put together a relay with some other
former Olympians, but even they couldn't beat the more

experienced solo swimmers. It took a different kind of body and spirit and I, Mr. Olympian-Wannabe, was thoroughly humbled.

But the most remarkable thing about this leg of the swim was how the water smelled. We were swimming downstream of the Upper West Side's water treatment plant, splashing around in its discharge. I could tell that we were in its waters by the sweet perfumey odor that clung to my lips and face. These days, most treatment plants' discharge is so well treated that many of their operators boast you can drink a glassful of it. Even so, I tried to keep as much out of my mouth as possible and focus on the task at hand. If I could just catch one of them, then at least I could reduce some of the shame. I picked up the pace.

Then a thunderstorm swept down upon us and they had to pull me out about one and a half miles shy of the finish. My time was almost up, and while I needed the break, the rest probably did me more harm than good. We stopped for more than an hour, and I shook violently the entire time, even though I was lying in the v-berth beside an electric space heater beneath half a dozen blankets. With each passing minute, I grew more and more tired. All-body spasms would come over me in waves and every time I thought they'd quit, another would hit me.

I was determined to finish my leg and I jumped back in when the storm had passed. I was less than a mile from the finish when my time was up, and they asked me if I wanted to take it home. The very question seemed to confirm my return to the fold. Flattered, I signaled I could make it, although my left leg was entirely numb. I had gained on the Australian woman a tad more and desperately wanted to catch her. Try as I did, though, she managed to elude me.

The guys were cheering and waving frantically as I got near Battery Park City's south cove — the finish line. Realizing it wasn't out of anger or fear but was actually because they were cheering me on, I lifted my head above the water so I could bask in their admiration and inspiration: "Swim, Forrest, swim!" the wags chanted.

Ah, all was right with the world.

I finished third in a time of 8:38. The four-man team from New York was first in 8:35 and the Australian woman finished in 8:36.

I stumbled ashore, waved with my arm held barely above my waist to the boat, and acknowledged the crowd, which was mistaking me for a solo swimmer. I then happily let Karel's and George's gorgeous wives lead me to the recovery table. I couldn't really talk and I didn't feel cold — very bad signs, given that I was shaking uncontrollably and half numb. It took five beautiful women, including the said wives, to massage me back to life. When I suggested they get under the space-age reflector blanket with me, naked, I knew I was getting better.

They declined.

Eleven

Like Learning How to French-Kiss in Beverly Smith's Closet

I had flagrantly failed in front of five knowledgeable swimmers, creating yet again that much-needed scenario where I had something to prove. I wallowed in the post-race ribbing that ensued, memorizing every little joke and jab at my expense. After we had a quick meal outside at a nearby café, George and Karel walked with me to the nearest avenue and even helped me hail a cab. They both offered to ride with me to a friend's house just so I wouldn't take the cab to my car and then attempt to drive home. It was as if I was their geriatric, enfeebled grandfather.

It was perfect.

Once again, I'd boxed myself in. The one thing I learned the past few years was that life threw many obstacles in the way of a forty-five-year-old man who was trying to compete in a younger man's sport. Every day presented a different legitimate reason to give up, to put aside the "wild and crazy" quest that was oh so endearing ("But seriously, Hodding, what are you really doing," the cocktail-party ladies liked to ask). To stay "on subject," keep my "eye on the prize," or whatever other helpful little phrase we use to suggest a focused approach, I had to construct walls that kept me from quitting. Some were positive: it's healthy, I was sort of getting paid for it, and I was setting a good example. Others, like having something to prove, weren't all that positive but they were probably even better for maintaining my focus.

Whatever the case, this most recent venture (I won't call it a failure) and all the others accumulated since 2004 created within me a calcified, unbreakable will. It became my Kenyon experience all over again. Lots of good times, utter embarrassment (then: quitting midrace in my freshman intra-squad meet on account of unwittingly having mono; now: the New York swim and all those other races where I didn't live up to my own expectations), and eventually an undeniable need to make something out of it all.

When I first started back, I used to waver a lot. I'd go for a few months and then get sidetracked by large and small events. I was like any other grown-up vowing to get in shape and lose fifteen pounds. Although I meant every word I said, I couldn't stay focused, and there was always a good reason. I hadn't had my back to the wall, but after

New York, I was pressed flat against it. I had no choice but to push back and stick with it to the very end.

Oddly, it became paradoxically liberating. I suddenly felt free to practice every day of the week. There was only one year left and I had much to do. After all, I still hadn't qualified for the Trials.

I dispensed with any swimming that wasn't going to improve my sprinting. In fact, I probably took it a little too far. On my sprint/power days, I did only short sprints or repeats on the Power Rack. I warmed up not by swimming easy laps in the pool but by lifting weights upstairs in the YMCA's weight room. I didn't want to do any slow swimming, worried it might imprint the wrong muscle memory. On my recovery days, instead of doing what most other sprinters might, some nontaxing endurance-based repeats with focused stroke work, I went to the extreme of not doing anything at all, beyond the few laps I covered while teaching swim lessons.

Over a series of months, I grew stronger and buffer than ever. I could finally bench more than two hundred pounds. I could do three sets of jump squats with sixty-five-pound dumbbells in each arm. In the pool, I could pull/lift seventy pounds in 6.2 seconds on the Power Rack. Still, I needed to race in an Olympic-length pool, having missed the two opportunities to do so in New England earlier in the summer, so I flew down to the Woodlands, Texas, with Mike Schmidt, Mike Ross, Beth Fries, and Bill Rupert for the 2007 Masters Long Course Nationals.

Although it wasn't really time for me to peak, I went there knowing I was going to win the 50 free and fly for my brand-new age category, 45 – 49.

❖ ❖ ❖

The five of us shared one room at the Woodlands Convention Center hotel—a rambling array of buildings strewn around the planned-community's famous golf course. The accommodations were similar in size and comfort to your average Holiday Inn, so we felt even closer after the weekend was over—but not any poorer thanks to Mike Schmidt.

Since quitting the law firm he worked for in Waterville, Maine, Mike had structured his family's economy on World Bank guidelines for debtor nations, and within months, his family lived on a fraction of their previous spending. Not including mortgage, his family spent little more than a thousand dollars a month—total. That included winter heating costs, food, insurance, gas, medical, and so on. His control over spending was so exemplary and well known that Lisa and I often would say aloud right before the other was about to make an impulse buy, "What would Mike do?"

I could also have asked myself that question regarding swimming, too, referring to either Mike Schmidt or Mike Ross. They both had a strong meet. Mike Schmidt swam some of his best times since returning to swimming in 2003 and he won the 200 fly in a gutsy, come-from-behind grind. I could literally see his arms and shoulders stiffen with lactic acid yet he still found a way to swim nearly two seconds faster on the last lap than the guy he beat by only five-tenths. Mike Ross, while not swimming as fast as he had in recent years, swam exceedingly well. Although he didn't beat any of his world records, he did win three of his races. They both swam with finesse, their speed coming more from style and body position than brute strength.

As for me, everything went as planned—for the first part of the race. I'd sharpened my reaction time to the starting horn by clapping my hands at the sound of the horn in some two-dozen heats before I swam. As a result, I was first off the blocks and a quarter-body length ahead at the start. I easily maintained my lead twelve seconds into the race at the 25-meter mark. All those sets on the Power Rack had paid off. I was still ahead at the 30, and then the 35. I remained in the lead at the 40, but then I did not so much shut down as sputter. By the 45, I was even with Steve Wood, a dentist from Dallas. I put my head down, determined not to breathe and thus slow my headway, but to no avail. Steve won, and by half a second. I'd died, something fierce.

While the two Mikes, although enviably fit, were mainly stroke technique and substance, I was Viagra Man. With my new hard body, I lacked style, substance, and definitely staying power. I couldn't ask how this could be; the answer was in the last few months of training. Despite my desire to will it so, training for 6.2 seconds at a time simply wasn't enough. I might have qualified for the 25-meter freestyle but there was no such event in the Olympics, or anywhere else, for that matter, if you were more than eight years old.

Although I set the New England records in the 50 free and 50 fly while down there, they weren't what made the trip so worthwhile. It was watching the two Mikes. I'd gathered all the pieces to my swimming puzzle; I just didn't know how to put them together. But watching them and listening to what they concentrated on revealed the clue I sorely needed: body position. I'd always paid lip service to these words, as expected of someone in my position (meaning a failed writer turned assistant aquatics instructor), but that had been it. Body position and perfect underwater technique were for people without enough power, not champs like me. (Really, that's what I truly thought and would've said if someone had pressed me to be honest.)

About ten days before Nationals, however, Marie Weferling, the long-time assistant coach of my Y's swim team and a full-time physician's assistant specializing in orthopedics, stopped me after a fast 25 sprint I'd just completed. I thought she was about to compliment me on my speed.

"Why do you do that?" she said. "Complete the underwater portion of your stroke so far past your suit?" (Translation: Why had my hand exited the water near the top of my thigh?)

Why? I wanted to scream. Why! Because it was how I swam, that's why! I'd been taught long, long ago to brush my thumb against my thigh as I was lifting my arm out of the water to make sure I was taking a full stroke. Everybody who knew anything about swimming knew you had to do this. Why would she even ask such a question and then stare at me with that I-can't-wait-to-see-what-is-going-to-come-out-of-his-mouth-this-time expression?

I started to answer angrily that a fast swimmer wouldn't ask such a thing when I suddenly and inexplicably knew better. I didn't stop myself out of kindness, but because the lightbulb finally lit up. I stammered a moment.

"I don't know," I said. "I guess because I always have."

Marie explained that Eddie Reese, the storied coach at the University of Texas at Austin, and other notable swim technicians thought that that flourish, a flourish that required years and years of weighted dips and triceps extensions to the point of collapse, was literally a waste of time. It was far better and more ergonomic to let my hand exit the water near the top of the waist—in other words, pull it out a lot sooner.

It was so close to Nationals. Making any change was risky. But the next day, I tried her suggestion and had to admit that I felt more efficient. And now bear with me as I try to explain this revolutionary change in stroke because it was crucial. By shortening my finish or upsweep or final push (whatever), I was able to do two things: recover my arms with a higher elbow and thus not swing them around to the front, which caused my hips to wag and my body to expend energy going sideways, and extend a little farther out in the beginning of the stroke. The latter occurred because my exit from the water was more dynamic and forward-moving. My hands naturally entered the water farther out front.

It was an unexpected breakthrough, I excitedly explained to Lisa that night as she scraped the plates, loaded the dishwasher, and scrubbed out the pasta-sauce pot. When she left the room, to empty the dehumidifier in the basement, I continued with Anabel and Eliza, who were taking turns reading the last Harry Potter book. When they fell asleep, making drool puddles I'd have to remember to wipe up later that night, I finished by explaining to Angus, who responded, "I don't want to sweep, Daddy."

Coming so close to the meet, this stroke change didn't necessarily help me out at Nationals in the 50, although perhaps it alone accounted for my dropping three-tenths of a second in the 50 free. It did, however, provide another piece of the puzzle. For the first time since returning to swimming—actually, for the first time ever—I started to question why I swam freestyle the way I did. Why was I doing any of the movements that I did? What was the reason behind the massive insweep that occurred more exaggeratedly with my left arm than my right? Why had I been stubbornly trying to swim with nearly straight arms on the underwater portion of the stroke?

Luckily, Fritz Homans walked into my life just about then. Fritz, a native of Bangor, had recently moved back to

Maine and enrolled his daughter in the age-group swim camp I'd hastily arranged for the week after Nationals. As far as swimming went, Fritz, a vice-president for a national vitamin company, was the real deal. He was the fastest swimmer that ever came out of the state of Maine, besides Ian Crocker (the current world-record holder in the 100-meter fly). More importantly, he'd dated Karlyn Pipes-Nielsen.

Karlyn is the winningest, most-record-settingest masters swimmer in the world. A wild partier in her youth, Karlyn sobered up in her thirties. She went back to college, which she had previously withdrawn from on account of her penchant for liquids a bit stronger than water, attending Cal State University, Bakersfield. While there she trounced her younger competition, setting Division II National titles like they were napkins on a table. Her current times, at the age of forty-five, were nearly as fast as the records she set back in her thirties, making her yet another perfect, feminine example of how we could age. Karlyn lived in Kona, Hawaii, where she surfed and made swimming videos.

One day, Fritz loaned me her video, thinking I might want to have her teach a clinic and perhaps hoping it'd give me a clue as to what I should teach the thirty-five campers we had at the Y. I'm not sure if it helped with the latter issue, but her DVD was about to change my life.

Seriously. I watched part of it one morning before the camp began and then I watched it again later that night, all the way through. And then I watched it again. Soon, it was the only thing I wanted to put on the TV or my computer to the chagrin of all four children.

"No, Daddy. No swim lady, Daddy," Angus would say.

"I hate you. You're so mean," Helen would add.

And then Anabel and Eliza would inexplicably start punching Helen.

Lisa had to stand in front of the screen, hands on hips, lips pinched tight together on more than one occasion.

I braved it all, though, simply to watch Karlyn swim.

I couldn't take my eyes off of her because she was swimming the way I should've been my entire life. Why hadn't anybody ever made a video like this before? Initially, her stroke, with its absurdly high elbows riding just beneath the surface of the pool, looked odd, a little comical even. Soon, though, her every move seemed to be cast in a golden aura. I knew this was how I should be swimming.

I started trying it in practice. Right off the bat, I was swimming with one less stroke per length of the pool without cheating (slowing down to glide more or pushing off farther underwater before beginning to swim).

As the weeks passed, I not only became more convinced that this was what I should be doing, but also that with a few tweaks, it represented the ultimate freestyle. One afternoon, as I yet again attempted to maintain a high elbow with my left arm as I breathed on my right side, I flicked my right hip a sharp 180 degrees down so my right arm could enter the water in front of me just as my left arm was beginning the catch phase of the stroke. It was such a eureka moment that I actually stopped swimming in the middle of the pool. It was an amazing, life-altering event—like learning how to French-kiss in Beverly Smith's closet.

This was what everybody had been talking about in bits and pieces. By trying to maintain Karlyn's high elbows even while breathing, I had to pause just long enough so that both arms were somewhere out in front of me before beginning one arm's underwater phase of the stroke, implementing a form of freestyle that USA Swimming had been pushing for quite a while called the Front Quadrant Stroke. To keep this pause from being interminably long, I had to flick my hip down on the side where the hand was just entering the water—just as Jon Olsen down at the Race Camp had practically begged me to do. I had to drive my hips hard with my core, relying nearly as much on all those central muscles as my shoulders and arms. This was something the Somax group charged five thousand dollars a week to teach people.[1] And in attempting to have the bottom half of my arm bent at ninety degrees to the pool's surface before my hand passed my shoulders, my head was forced down so it felt as if I was "swimming downhill"—the catchphrase of many modern coaches   and my lats, not my shoulders, powered the

---

1. Well, I think that's what they're teaching among other things, based on what I've gleaned from their Web site. They run swim camps and I'd considered going there when I opted for the Race Club. I would gladly have racked up another huge sum on my credit card if Lisa would've let me.

stroke, just as all those fishlike Aussies had been doing in the early nineties.

When taken alone, all of these disparate suggestions and techniques helped a person swim freestyle well, but when combined, they were a potent force, creating what I now saw was the überstroke.

The only problem was that I, a tired but game forty-five-year-old Walter Mitty, was the one who'd pieced it all together. Maybe Karlyn had as well, but she never actually came out and said, *Take all these steps in this sequence and you will be swimming freestyle as it was always meant to be swum.*

I fired off e-mails to Mike Ross and my camp buddy, John Fields, bubbling with the zealotry of the newly saved. (I skipped over Mike Schmidt not out of competitiveness but simply because I knew he'd be more skeptical and level-headed. I didn't want any reining in — still don't, for that matter.) I directed them to YouTube footage of Ian Thorpe and Grant Hackett swimming taken from an underwater viewpoint. I pleaded with them to buy Karlyn's DVD.[2]

✺ ✺ ✺

2. I realize much of the last few pages has been a bit technical and perhaps even confusing, and for that I apologize. It was such a major breakthrough, though, that I had to share and explain it for anyone who might want to improve their freestyle

Since this all happened a few months ago, I hadn't, by the close of this story, had the proper venue to prove the stroke's supremacy. Mike Ross said he couldn't quite get the hang of the hip movement, didn't understand the hip flicking, but after talking to him about the stroke, I watched underwater footage of him swimming. His stroke, perhaps without his knowing it, was almost exactly like what I'd been training myself to do. About the only thing he didn't do quite in step was the hip rotation, which appeared to occur a fraction of a second too late.

Once I saw he was already swimming close to the über-stroke, I started watching underwater footage of any fast, modern swimmer I could track down on the Internet, and nearly all of them were swimming this way, except for a major variation practiced by many Australian swimmers that involves—well, okay, maybe you don't need to know everything I learned.[3]

---

as well. I looked at video footage of Mike Ross and many of the world's great swimmers and they all swim this way to one extent or another, except for a major variation practiced by many Australian swimmers that involves—well, okay, maybe you don't need to know everything I learned. But in case you do: pull the elbow and humerus, the upper arm bone, that is, toward your side after the catch phase of the stroke, making your arm swing shut to your side, like a door. Still confused? Watch Ian Thorpe underwater on YouTube.

3. But in case you do: pull the elbow and humerus, the upper arm bone, toward your side, in effect making it swing shut like a door.

I'm convinced this change can bring me Olympic glory or, barring that, at least a chance to compete at the Olympic Trials. It isn't as long of a shot as it was when I first started trying to make the trials back in 2004. I have gotten faster every step of the way, and older swimmers like Dara Torres and Paul Carter, it is clearly possible, even for a less-competent competitor like me.

Yet, given the amount of time I have before the trials begin, now just seven months away as I write this, I know it might not happen.

But there's always 2012.

As long as my wife and kids can stand it, I don't see any reason why I shouldn't continue to train like an elite sprinter. Not only am I in the best shape of my life at age forty-five, but there are also other, more intangible benefits to what I'm doing. Lisa and I get along better now than we have in years because I'm both happy and satisfied. I've been happy many times in my life, but satisfied? Hardly ever. I've always been striving, wanting more, thinking that if I could just do x, then I'd be okay.

Some might think that by having the Olympics as a goal I couldn't be satisfied, but that would be missing the whole point. It is this very act of trying, embracing a challenge to its fullest extent, that has me living in the moment for the first time in a very long time. Although I have a goal that I hope to achieve in the future, it's right now that matters—what I do each and every day. I'm truly happy being Hodding, that guy everybody knows is trying to do the impossible, that guy who refuses to believe that age matters. Some people may laugh at me. I don't care.

These days, all I need is a body of water and my day is good. This swimming thing is all I ever really wanted. Now, it's what I do. Who I am. I haven't felt this way since I was a kid. And maybe, I still am that kid—with a startlingly wrinkly face.[4]

---

4. As of December 18, 2007, I had just returned from the most recent New England Championships. I dropped a half second off my 50 and am within one-tenth of my best time ever. I have seven months until the trials. I am going to make it.

Twelve

The Smile

That's not how this story ends, though, as it leaves out an ever-expanding part of my life: coaching. I not only allowed Jason to "trick" me into working full-time at his old job as assistant aquatics director in April 2007 but I also willingly became the YMCA's new swim coach. I acquired this position much like I do everything else in life, on a whim. Anabel, Eliza, and Helen were all on the team, so why not coach it?

Currently, I can think of sixty-nine reasons not to. That's how many swimmers (sixty-five) and coaches (four) I have. A person reading this book might wonder how I can continue to believe that I can make the 2008 Olympic team, but what amazes me more is the presumption that I could coach the Penobscot Bay Sailfish just because I knew a little bit about swimming. I'm constantly in over my head—and I'm not just saying that for the aquatic imagery. I'm almost literally in over my head when a coach from another team intentionally bumps me at my first championship swim meet; I am literally in over my head when some of the little brats, I mean swimmers, push me in the pool after our last home meet; and I'm figuratively in over my head on a constant basis. Take, for example, the scene at the Casco Bay YMCA pool during a recent winter swim meet.

I am on the deck hovering over two lanes where my entire travel team of fifty-three swimmers is trying to warm up for the meet. If the kids were to hold on to each other hands to feet, they would fill the lanes twice over, it is so crowded; yet, I'm supposed to keep them moving and well organized enough to be ready to race in fifteen minutes. Marie—the same Marie who has been helping me with my stroke—oversees the lane next to me while occasionally glaring (I believe) at me for being late. Fritz, whom I have talked into helping me coach, is trying to keep his seven-year-old son Harry from doing faceplants off a starting block while impressing upon a five-year-old the importance of stopping at the end of his race instead of continuing on like he did the last two times he competed. Casey, who should be here to warm up half the kids, has just called to say that she's late because she's slid her car into a ditch.

I look down into the lane and a senior swimmer has just run over two of the younger swimmers, who apparently stopped midlane during a sprint set. They've come up, gasping for air, and one of them is crying. The older swimmer is trying to apologize when another swimmer runs into him while doing backstroke. Within seconds, the scene resembles a ten-car pileup on a California freeway and a lifeguard is yelling at me to get my swimmers off the lane line.

That's when Jane,[1] chair of my team's parent board, decides to approach me about an event I've put her son in. She wants to know why he's swimming the 50 back instead of the 100 free. "There's no 50 back for his age group at States. He can't qualify for New Englands or Nationals in this race; he's too old. Why is he signed up for this? I didn't drive all the way here to watch him swim in a race that doesn't matter," she says, all in one breath.

I actually have a lot of reasons—some good ones, even—for putting him in this race. His body is tired because I've been piling on the intense training lately and so he has no chance of making qualifying times in his important races. I think sprinting backstroke is an important complement to sprinting freestyle (his major stroke). He is a good backstroker and it's important to work on his speed. And I didn't know he was trying to qualify for New Englands in the 100 free. For these reasons and others, I have put him in the 50 back. But do I think of all these things at that very second? No, of course not.

So I respond, "Because I wanted him to," and I turn

---

1. This isn't her real name. I don't think I'm writing about her in an unflattering manner, but then again, my judgment is questionable; after all, I still think I'm going to qualify for the trials.

back to the pool. She doesn't leave. She's tall, around six feet, and she's towering and glowering beside me. There's a team rule that parents aren't allowed on the deck during a meet. Given her position on the parent board and the fact that she works at most of our meets, she's usually not affected by this rule, but this is an away meet. She doesn't have a reason to be on the deck besides getting mad at me. So I blurt out, "Get off the deck."

She doesn't budge.

"Get off the deck," I repeat, turning toward her for the first time. Her brow is furrowed and she actually looks mad. For some reason, perhaps because it seems so out of proportion, this infuriates me. "Parents are not supposed to be on the pool deck. Get away from me!" I even go so far as to utter a cuss word — but at least not directly at her.

Her eyes widen, she blanches and strides away.

Momentarily, I'm elated, feeling that same joy a rebellious kid feels when he's mouthed off to his parents, and then, of course, I realize what I've done. Just as quickly, I'm deflated, as all the reasons why I shouldn't have exploded come to me, first and foremost being that a gentleman doesn't talk that way to a lady. I was raised in the South and part of me still believes I'm supposed to be a gentleman, despite my repeated failures at doing so.

Of course, not all my coaching moments have been so despicable. Jane and I have since made up and nearly all of my interactions with parents have been wonderful. There is, however, some sense of mania that I'd love to lose or at least lessen, but doing so has escaped me so far. My coaching and swimming are bound together, hurtling toward some moment in the future where all will become clear, or at least resolved.

I've become just as obsessed with teaching proper freestyle as I am with swimming fast. I lose my voice in practice yelling at the kids to snap their hips in place while they look up at me with blank faces, dismissive chuckles, and occasionally smiles of comprehension. And on the way from the pool office to the bathroom, I often stop by the lanes and give unsolicited advice to lap swimmers. It used to drive me a little crazy when Dolly, the seventy-something butterflier who always corrects my stroke, would do this to me, but I find I can't help myself. I'm literally bursting with enthusiasm and advice on swimming.

A couple of days ago I stopped by a lane where this fit guy in a Speedo was doing some sprint freestyle. Without even giving it a second thought, I stuck a kickboard into the water just as he was about to execute another lousy flipturn.

As he glanced up at me (or was it a grimace), trying to catch his breath, I informed him, "You're crossing your centerline when your hands enter the water and then when you initiate the catch phase of your stroke—you know what I mean, when you start to pull on the water, slightly bending your wrist—you're bending your wrist too much. And you need to keep your elbows up higher in the power phase of the stroke while flicking your hip into place, because your hips and core have a lot more power than your puny triceps and shoulder will ever have. And then try to sweep your upper arm toward your side, pretending that your arm is a door that you're trying to shut and then end with your fingertips still pointing down—not toward your feet like you're doing—exiting the water at your hip, not your thigh. See, what you need to do is pretend that your body is like a pig on a spit. There's a pole going from end to end through your center. You want your body to rotate or pivot on this pole as you swim, not wiggle from side to side."

Before he had a chance to thank me, a swimmer in the lane next to him caught my attention. She was swimming butterfly, a commendable feat in its own right, but her butt was dragging way below the waterline and her head was coming way up high, like a dying seal gasping for air just as a shark dragged it deep below the surface. I tried to tell her not to let her butt sag, but she pushed off before I could finish.

Admittedly, I was feeling a bit rabid that day, but I still don't think I deserved two complaint cards.[2]

Until very recently, my favorite moments at the Y had come when I had a breakthrough in practice or did a best time. These days, it's when one of my swimmers has an "aha!" moment, like when thirteen-year-old Ellery managed to keep her head down while breathing when doing butterfly. I had been trying to get her to do it properly for a few weeks but it hadn't sunk in. Then one day, when she

---

2. I used to like the complaint/suggestion box at the Y before I started working there.

was tired and her head hung low in the water, I pointed it out to her. Something about noticing she was doing it the right way while tired helped her to retain the ability to do it at will. Ever since, she's been swimming fly with a lower profile, helping her to move forward instead of up and down.

My most cherished experiences coaching, though, have come with my own girls. Just this past weekend, I endured my first Maine State YMCA Swimming Championships as a coach. It was the most grueling swim meet I've ever been to and I've got the sore back, aching legs, and raspy sore throat to prove it. All this pain and I didn't race a single lap.

I'd heard that States was the true test of a coach's spirit—that if you came out the other end of one of these weekends and still wanted to coach, you'd found your calling. In the beginning of the season, I'd successfully pushed thoughts of this weekend out of mind and didn't start worrying about it until about a month ago, when all the forms, entries, etc., for the meet started to be due. It was then that I started to lose sleep at night and become testier and testier in practice. My solution was to pretend that it wasn't actually happening. Marie would ask me things like, "Hodding, have you asked for a check to pay for the teams' entries? It's due next Tuesday."

"Of course," I lied. "I not only asked for the check, I've already sent it in." Then, since this was a Friday, I ran upstairs and begged Ted (whose daughter, thank God, was on the team) if he could rush through a check for me without a purchase order. He saw the grown-man-about-to-blubber look on my face and cut me a check in a matter of minutes.

I kept putting the meet out of my mind because it didn't sound like fun. Not only would I not be swimming but the team would be divided into separate groups for racing. Each age group would be swimming all by itself. One of the things that made coaching so much fun was the energy gained from everybody cheering each other on and just being together at the meet. Also, this being the championship meet, many of the parents were suddenly showing a lot of interest in what their kids were swimming and, to make matters worse, a few of them didn't like what I'd chosen for their kids to race. Those entries were irreversible by the time the parents complained to me, so it was adding up to be a very uncomfortable time. Worst, I'd gone to the meet the previous year as a dad and still remembered the exhausted and horrified look on Jason's face—a week after the meet was over.

Here is what it was going to be like: Hours and hours of screaming and yelling—swimmers yelling for other swimmers, coaches yelling for swimmers, parents yelling for swimmers, parents yelling at coaches, who mercifully couldn't hear them because the parents were stuck up in the stands. The first day would last a total of fifteen hours without a single break. The eight-and-under swimmers would go first for four hours or so and then the nine- and ten-year-olds would begin warm-up the minute the younger kids were done, and so on. The other coaches and I would be there the entire time, warming the swimmers up, getting their times, psyching them up, consoling them, playing peacemaker, turning in scratch sheets, making protests when overzealous judges made calls that it would take a slowed-down and magnified instant replay to be able to honestly discern, etc. All the while, we'd be standing poolside on the hard tile deck hour after hour. Thus the sore legs mentioned earlier.

It sounded like torture and as the dreaded weekend got closer and closer, I was thinking I'd rather spend the day raking my fingernails across a blackboard than suffer through the state meet. What had I been thinking, saying I wanted to coach the team? I'd made practically every novice mistake a person could make and had boasted again and again that we had to, and were going to, do much better than last year's thirteenth-place showing, although I'd never, ever been a head coach.

In other words, the state meet was going to be awful.

Except, of course, I was wrong.

There are so many moments from the literally twenty-four-and-a-half hours of coaching that flash before me: (1) Ten-year-old Riley rearing back on the starting block before the 50 freestyle as if she were a mini Dara Torres and then flying through the air with the grace of an Olympic diver, when just a few months back she'd been a gangly, flailing mess who was more likely to be in need of rescue than to be crowned most improved; when the race was done, she'd dropped nearly twenty seconds since first joining the team last summer. (2) Eleven-year-old

Dimitri roaring through the water on his leg of the 200 freestyle relay to overcome the disqualification he'd caused by leaving his previous relay too early. (3) Casey lying passed out behind an overturned table in a musty hallway because she'd shown up to help coach the meet although she was suffering from a virulent form of the flu that was decimating our town. (4) My daughter Eliza's smile.

All of the girls had a great meet, Anabel and Helen especially so. Both Anabel and Helen were among the fastest swimmers on their trophy-winning relays and they both had significant time drops in their individual races. The two of them, however, had had a much easier year with the whole swimming thing. They were on the team because they loved swimming and in Helen's case, even loved working out. They would have been on the team whether or not I was the coach. Anabel's like a mad dog when she gets in a race, unwilling to let go until she's triumphed, and Helen would rather swim than do practically anything else. Her favorite book last year was Lynne Cox's *Swimming to Antarctica*.

Eliza, though, was only swimming for one reason: her dad was the coach. Without saying so, she was doing it so as not to let me down. Although she and Anabel are identical twins and they are equal in many things, it is no srecret that Eliza does not swim quite as quickly as Anabel (probably because of her ever-so-slighter build and not because of her strokes, which are the more elegant of the twins'). Coming into the meet, she was talking about quitting . . . until she swam her leg of the relay.

That's when, as Fritz says about breakthrough moments in swimming, something snapped.

I watched through one eye, actually wincing because I was afraid to see it, as she dove in for her leg of butterfly on the medley relay. She was swimming this difficult stroke not because she liked it but because I'd noticed her doing it well in practice. And so as I watched, I was already trying to figure out how to console her, but her stroke was incredibly smooth. To me, she looked like a flying fish, darting in and out of the water, first over and then below the waterline, streaking toward the wall. It was a swim of beauty.

It was her smile, though, the giant, irrepressible one that took over her face even before she was told her time (faster than she'd ever gone), that made me realize the weekend wasn't only about the drudgery and unending chaos. I'd been enjoying the days' races but Eliza's happiness made everything complete. I felt blessed to have three of my own kids deriving joy from the same sport that had been, and still was, such a large part of my life.

✿ ✿ ✿

I didn't start swimming in the winter of 2004 completely out of the blue, although I'd believed that I did for quite a while. Seeing Eliza smile after I told her how great her swim was reminded me that it all started because my girls were taking swim lessons. Originally, I wanted something to do to kill time while they were swimming.

Then, when they were thinking about joining the team, I wanted them to see that it was fun to do workouts. Then, when they stuck with competitive swimming, I wanted us all to be doing the same thing.

I realize now that under all the reasons, rationalizations, and layers of justification, the reason I'm doing any of this—coaching and swimming, that is—is for a certain picture I carry in my head. I once told a friend I was worried that I only wanted to be successful in life to draw attention to myself. That the only reason I was writing was because I wanted to be famous to compete with my father. That I just wanted to be noticed. He laughed when I said this and asked me to form a picture in my head of my ultimate goal.

Well, the picture wasn't a snapshot of me holding up rave reviews of my latest book. I wasn't surrounded by photographers or autograph-seekers. I wasn't in some luxurious home or hotel room. I didn't have gorgeous models at my feet or people fawning all over me. And I didn't even have an Olympic medal draped over my chest. The picture that instantly came to mind, perhaps to my own surprise and delight, was of my family. It was my wife, my four kids, and me, all broadly smiling, just like Eliza had smiled at the state meet.

APPENDIX

Typical Short Course Yard Workout

I've included this workout not because I'm some kind of genius workout writer, but in hopes that other swimmers will see that it takes very little yardage to swim fast. We've been brainwashed in this country to believe that a good workout means lots of yardage. I tried swimming that way the first few years after my return to swimming, doing up to seven thousand yards at a go, but I didn't get the results I wanted. (I sucked.) After going to Gary Hall's swim camp, talking with Mike Schmidt (the king of writing/ creating workouts), and much trial and error, I decided that less was indeed more. What follows is my typical hard-day workout. I do it three times a week, on the same day I lift weights.[1] The other two or three days a week that

---

1. I do the same lifting routine practiced by Kenyon College's sprinters that I learned during my week swimming there in the fall of 2006. I lift for about an hour, mixing in plyometric work on my legs and shoulders/lats with some basic free-weight lifting. I usually do three sets with fifteen to twenty reps, working toward failure on each set. Otherwise the only interesting thing I

I train, I do the same amount of yardage but at no greater than 80 percent effort. On those days, I work more on technique, starts and turns, and maintaining aerobic conditioning—meaning I swim just hard enough to raise my heart rate to 130–150 bpm for fifteen minutes or so.

Ever since making the changes to my freestyle suggested by Karlyn Pipes-Nielsens' video and doing these types of workouts, I started swimming fast. As of this writing, I'm number one in the country for my age for the 50 freestyle, the 100 freestyle, and the 50 butterfly in the short course meter venue, but by the time you read this I will have qualified for the Olympic Trials at the age of forty-five. All because of these low-yardage but high-intensity workouts.

So, ignore my training advice at your own risk. The only thing that could make you swim faster is growing longer feet and hands. The one thing that nearly all elite swimmers have in common is long feet; in their world, size-twelve feet is considered small.

---

do is focus on strengthening and increasing the flexibility of my core. I both love and hate those brightly colored, ubiquitous-in-the-health-club exercise balls that are the bane of all soft, apple-pie lovin' stomachs.

1. 200 warm-up

2. 10 x 50 freestyle with a snorkel on a :45 interval, focusing on distance per stroke (DPS)

The point here is to improve stroke power for each arm, work on body position, and streamline. I do an almost catch-up stroke—a freestyle technique known as front quadrant swimming. This allows for a longer waterline— one arm is almost always extended forward—which means more possible speed for a displacement-type vessel, such as a boat or a human body.

I use the snorkel so I can work on my body position. Not having to think about breathing to the side, I'm able to rotate my hips equally and really concentrate on getting my head and chest down, arm placement, etc. I can't say enough about how useful the snorkel is for improving technique.

3. All-out freestyle for 1:45 with parachute and paddles

The easiest way to get faster in swimming is by improving power and/or technique. The previous set (10 × 50) and others like it work on technique. This set is all about power. After a few years back in the pool I realized that I couldn't make any real power gains unless I added resistance training. Pulling an eight-inch diameter nylon parachute feels roughly equal to pulling forty pounds of deadweight through the water. I wear the paddles because they make me push more water than normal, which also causes my muscles to work harder.

My goal time for the 200-yard freestyle these days is a 1:45. In this set, I try to go as far as I can, hoping to make 200 yards sometime in the near future—a near impossibility since the parachute and paddles make me go about four seconds slower every fifty yards. Each week I get closer and closer, so I know I am making gains. When I first started doing this set, I could go 137 yards or so. Now—four months later—I can go 150. This is done all out and my arms and legs fill with lactic acid by 1:30 or so.

4. Easy 100

5. 2 x 100 with parachute and paddles

Again, these are at near 100-percent effort and there is no interval. I usually rest three to four minutes between each 100—long enough to willingly try it one more time.

6. Easy 100

(Because by now, you're dying.)

7. 4 x 50 with parachute and paddles

I either do these on a one-minute interval—getting both anaerobic and aerobic benefits—or on a two-and-a-half minute interval, for more anaerobic improvement.

8. Easy 100

9. 10 x 50 kick on 1:00

These are done with a board and every other one is all out. Not much of my freestyle's speed comes from the kick, but every little bit helps.

10. 500 freestyle with snorkel

I like to end the workout by reinforcing proper technique, especially focusing on good hip usage and rotation.

Total yards: 2,600

ACKNOWLEDGMENTS

I've pretty much acknowledged everybody I need to within the pages of this book, although I have not properly bowed down before my wife and begged her forgiveness. I've made it painfully clear that she is the superior being, but is that really enough? And what could I say here that makes it clear how much greater a spouse she is than all other spouses of muddling writers and wannabe Olympians in not only America but the entire world? So, all I can think to say, in advance, is this: I dedicate my Olympic gold medal to you, Lisa. Want to see my muscles?

In the same breath, I'd also like to thank my, in her words, "very kind editor," Kathy Pories. Yes, I tuned in a ner-perfect manusciprt to here, widout singel a word misspled or misplaced but still she done a purty goode job: all in all. If you enjoy this book to any degree, it's all her doing. I just wish she'd work on her patience.

And to Sally Wofford-Girand, my agent: Okay, I'll make it 50 percent. Thanks ever so much.

And thank you *Best Life* for sending me to swim camp when my parents wouldn't come through.